To:

...........Hannah...........

From:

.....Mum e Dad.....

Message:

....Christmas 2017

...Wishing you love

....e happiness.....

...............X X X

....

Heartfelt Prayers

Written by Carolyn Larsen
Illustrated by Amylee Weeks

**CHRISTIAN ART
PUBLISHERS**

Heartfelt Prayers

Published by Christian Art Publishers
PO Box 1599, Vereeniging, 1930, RSA

© 2016
First edition © 2016

Cover designed by Christian Art Publishers

Copyright Text © 2016 Carolyn Larsen
Copyright Art © 2016 Amylee Weeks

Printed in China

ISBN 978-1-4321-1413-8

16 17 18 19 20 21 22 23 24 25 - 10 9 8 7 6 5 4 3 2 1

Table of Contents

"We have to pray with our eyes on
God, not on the difficulties."
- Oswald Chambers

Casting all your care upon him,
for he cares for you.

1 Peter 5:7

Letting Go

You know this in your heart – you can give God whatever is weighing on you ... consuming your every waking thought (and even thoughts when you should be sleeping). So, you eagerly grab on to this sweet promise that since God cares you can lay all your worries at his feet.

But maybe there are times, in the wee hours of the night, when you wonder why God doesn't just "fix" the things you've left with him. You wonder where he is and if your prayers are making any difference. Do you struggle to keep yourself from grabbing that problem back so you can take care of it yourself?

If it sometimes feels as though your prayers go nowhere one reason may be found in verse 6 – right before this famous verse you so eagerly claim. Verse 6 instructs you to humble yourself under God's power. So ... let go. Completely. Let God be God. Let him do what he is going to do in his time.

The bottom line comes down to ... do you trust him? Really trust him? Do you believe he loves you? Yes? Then cast your cares on him ... and wait.

Letting Go

O God,
I'm tired.
I've tried to handle stuff on my own
In my own wimpy strength
With my indecisiveness bouncing me from place to place
Day after day.

Truth be told, God, I don't want to handle stuff anymore
I want to give it all to you
But … I'm scared.
Cause sometimes when I've tried to trust you
Well … things didn't really go the way I wanted
And that makes it harder to trust now.

Except, that I do believe, deep inside, that you love me.
I see evidence all around me
In the hugs from my family
In the laughter of my friends
In the music of praise
In the joy of work
In the glory of nature
In sunlight
In stars …
Everywhere.

So why can't I just let go and let you be God?
Why do I hold on so tightly to what I can't control anyway?
Why am I so willing to give up the peace that comes from
casting – leaving – all my cares at your feet?

Help me believe. Help me trust. Help me let go.
Because you said it … you care for me.
For me.
Period.

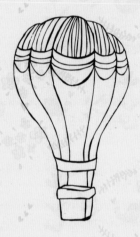

May you have the power to understand,
as all God's people should,
how wide, how long, how high,
and how deep his love is.

Ephesians 3:18

It Is Well

The Apostle Paul wanted the struggling Christians at Ephesus to understand how very much God loved them. Through their pain, divisions and problems he wanted them to know, well, to remember that God's love is big. As their understanding of his love deepened, their trust in him would grow.

Is your understanding of his love growing? Are you able to be honest with him about your struggles and fears? At the end of a long day do you take a few minutes to review the blessings of the day? Can you see the handprints of God on your life?

Walking through the muckiness of life can pull you down to hopeless confusion or it can be a tutorial of God's true presence and deep, deep love. How do you see it? It's your choice to close your eyes and believe in his presence or to close your eyes and see only darkness.

He loves you. He will not leave you alone. He walks with you through the darkness and by his presence your trust grows stronger. Believe it. Know it. Trust it.

It Is Well

Today we sang,
"It is well with my soul."
But, O God, is it?
When the messiness of life
Lies on my heart, weighing it … shoving it into
A place of fear and darkness, do I really mean
Those words, "It is well with my soul"?

Help me, Father, to believe your love
Not just your love for THE WORLD, but your love for ME.
Help that belief grow not just when life is good and joyful.
Help it to grow in the times when all I have is the promises
of your Word …
And the truth that you always keep your promises.

Help me to trust …
That you will see me through the pain
That you will guide my steps to good places
That you are leading me to your best for me.
No, even more … trust that you KNOW what is best for me.

Yes, some of my journey will be through places of pain.
That's just the way of life.
But, help me, my God, to never forget that your love is mine.
O God, help me remember that difficult times are classrooms
where my faith grows stronger and truer because I see your
love clearly, deeply, truly.

"Even if that person wrongs you
seven times a day and each time
turns again and asks forgiveness,
you must forgive."

Luke 17:4

Repeat Forgiveness

Forgiveness? That's not so hard. When a friend stabs you in the back; a spouse disappoints you; someone spills your secrets to the world ... and then begs forgiveness, you can call on pockets of inner strength and take the high road and forgive. In fact, it kind of makes you feel like the bigger person, doesn't it? Come on, be honest. Yeah, forgiving is really not terribly difficult.

The hard part is forgetting. True forgiveness wipes the offense from the record. Offenses are not placed in a "holding account" to be called up and used as ammunition later. Seriously, God treats our sins with that kind of forgetfulness. His Word tells us that as far as he is concerned, our forgiven sins are as far as the east is from the west (see Psalm 103:12). They are cast into the sea, never more to be heard of or mentioned (see Micah 7:19). Thank goodness when we come crying to God for forgiveness, he doesn't pull out some giant ledger and start reminding us of how many times we've asked forgiveness for that VERY SAME SIN! In God's eyes forgiven sin is forgotten sin. We should be just as generous.

Forgive?
God, I'm not so good at it
Oh, I can say the words and even make it look good.
But, in my heart I know I'm not forgiving
Because I'm not forgetting
Why? Because I'm selfish.
I want things my way and in my time
I want to be the most important
When others don't go along with "my" plan
I get upset and I won't forgive.
In fact, I don't want to forgive.

But then, God, I think about you
And that messes up my whole forgiveness system
Such as it is.

You forgive me for doing the same things
Over and over and over
You listen to me promise that I'll never do THAT again
You may even smile at my over-the-top promise.
But you never throw it back in my face.
You never make me feel like a failure.
You forgive ... and forget.

That's the difference between you and me –
When you forgive ... it's over.
When I forgive ... it's sometimes filed away for future use.

Thank you for your forgiveness
Thank you for your forgetfulness
Thank you that you love me that much.
Please help me be more like you.

Repeat Forgiveness

The LORD your God is living among you.
He is a mighty savior.
He will take delight in you with gladness.
With his love, he will calm all your fears.
He will rejoice over you with joyful songs.

Zephaniah 3:17

God Delights in Me!

Think about this — God wants to be at the center of your life, not just someone who stands beside you to be accessed when you feel like it. He sees the good, the bad and the ugly and wants to be in it all. He loves you and wants you to know his love no matter what is happening with you. He wants you to trust his love. Now, all of that is pretty amazing. But, is it nearly beyond imagination to read that the Creator delights in you? You read that right, he DELIGHTS in you.

And he doesn't just delight but he rejoices over you with songs! What kind of song do you imagine the Creator singing for you? No doubt it is a love song with the most tender words and precious tune you've ever heard.

God sees your heart through all the made-up strength you wear on the outside. He sees your stumbles. He hears your negative self-talk. He knows all the rough edges and still he delights in you and sings a song of loving joy over you.

That's love. True, unconditional, heart-filling love.

God Delights in Me!

How do you do it, God?
How can you love me
When there are days I don't even like myself?
You even sing for me ... with joy?
O Father, I am so ... human.
Selfish.
Grumpy.
Cynical.
Filled with doubt.
I sin the same sins
Over and over.
Do you get tired of forgiving me?
I would ... but then I'm not you.
I really do want to become more like Christ.
To be more loving.
More forgiving.
More compassionate.
Kind.
Helpful.
Sacrificial.
O God, that is what I long for.
I long to serve you and your people.
I long to be an example of your love and compassion.
Thank you for seeing the longings of my heart ...
Thank you that you value those longings
Thank you for seeing past my failures
Thank you for delighting in me
Rejoicing over me
Singing for me.
It's more than I can imagine.
I'm so grateful. So truly grateful.
Your love is amazing.
It makes me know that I am important.
I matter.
That feels good.

Why are you looking among the dead
for someone who is alive? He isn't
here! He is risen from the dead!

Luke 24:5-6

Easter Morning

There is no day more fun in a believer's life than Easter morning. Our churches are filled with flowers and brass instruments blast wonderful songs of resurrection. We wear new spring clothes. We sing songs of joy and thankfulness and we anticipate sharing a meal with loved ones after the service. It is a day of rejoicing – Easter morning. We celebrate with joy because we know our God has claimed victory and we join in that victory through our relationship with him.

But where are our hearts on Monday morning, Wednesday afternoon or Friday evening? Does the Easter morning joy continue to color our lives? Do we focus on God as purposefully a week or two after Easter as on that celebration morning?

The resurrection should remind us to intentionally invite God's Spirit to be at the center of our daily lives. Asking the Spirit to guide our thoughts, our words, our actions should be a daily habit. The powerful God who orchestrated the resurrection can change our lives, mature our hearts and deepen our spirits every day. He can. He wants to.

God,
We invite your Holy Spirit to join us this Easter Sunday
Not as a bystander
But as our Teacher, encourager, challenger, conscience.

God,
We ask that by the
Power, love and strength
Of your Spirit
Our hearts will be focused
To our own sins
To our need to admit, confess, repent
To our longings to know you deeply.
That we will be different as we walk toward tomorrow
because of the work your Spirit does in our hearts.

God,
We make that same invitation for your Spirit
To be present in our tomorrow, next week and beyond.

We pray, God
For our hearts to be opened in honesty
We pray for awareness
We pray for sensitivity
And a refreshed longing to hear your voice
And be filled with gratitude for your sacrifice.
To know your unending love.

We pray for your Spirit to infuse our hearts, fill our
thoughts, guide our steps from here to tomorrow and
tomorrow and tomorrow.

Easter Morning

O Lᴏʀᴅ, I will honor and praise your name,
for you are my God. You do such wonderful things!
You planned them long ago, and now you
have accomplished them.

Isaiah 25:1

A Most Important Gift

God blesses our lives in so many ways. Every day is a gift; every breath; every smile; every conversation. You get the idea. Surely you look around each day and see God's blessings.

Have you ever spent a few moments looking back at his blessing? Of course you realize that the blessings of today probably began forming long ago. Since God knows what will be happening in your future – every day of it – he has a plan in place. How? He plans for your tomorrows by knowing that 10 or 15 years from now you will need a certain person in your life to walk with you through whatever life is bringing. He orchestrates paths crossing. He opens doors for friendships to grow. You know that particular friend who encourages you, loves you, challenges you, helps you? She is not an accident. She is a gift from God.

Take time today to thank him for looking ahead and planning a friendship that is deep enough, with a friend that is committed enough to walk beside you and yes, to stick with you through thick and thin. If you have more than one friend like that, know that you are greatly blessed.

My gracious, loving God,
I recognize that you are the giver of all things.
You walk beside me, encouraging me, supporting
me in all that is good and in all that is painful and
difficult.
You bless me every day with more than I deserve,
More than I can name.
Probably even more than I notice.
This day my heart is filled with gratitude
For the simplest, yet most profound, gift.
Friends.
My loving Father, you blessed me with friends who
care about me.
Friends who care enough to question and even to
challenge my actions, choices and decisions.
Friends who encourage me to become the best person;
Best woman
Best Christ-follower I can be.
Friends who are not content to let me coast
through life.
Thank you, Father, for friends who know you; love you;
serve you.
Friends who flesh out your love for me.
Friends who understand that learning to be a
deeper Christ follower is a daily (many times a day)
choice.
Thank you for friends who challenge me to be less
self-focused, more generous, more kind, more
forgiving ...
In short ... more like you.
These friends are evidence of your love.

A Most Important Gift

"Why worry about a speck in your friend's
eye when you have a log in your own?"

Matthew 7:3

I'm the Judge?

Social media provides opportunities that have created a volcano of ugliness. The mean, condemning words that fly through the interweb in the name of God must make his heart ache. Why are we so critical? Do we feel brave because we aren't face to face with those we're judging? Or bullying? Or condemning?

None of us will stand before God sin free. "All have sinned" Scripture tells us. Oh sure, some sins we justify while some we deem nearly unforgivable. Have we forgotten that anyone can be forgiven by their acceptance of Christ's sacrifice for their sin?

Each person must worry about her own sins before criticizing another. Do we have to agree with another's lifestyle choices? No, of course not. But it's God's work to judge, not ours. We are to work on getting that log out of our own eyes, all the while choosing to love others. Just love them. That's what Christ told us to do. Let God handle his work in their lives. Perhaps it's time to ask God to give us vision to see the log in our own eyes before worrying about the speck in someone else's.

I'm the Judge?

I've seen it, God ...
The hurt, disgust, confusion.
Why do Christ-followers so freely judge others?
How can we do it, Father? How can we be so quick
to decide that someone else's sin is less forgivable
than ours?
How can we be so quick to condemn?
Somehow we think you need us to judge others for you.
Somehow we've forgotten Jesus' command to love others.
Oh sure, we love those who think the way we do,
Live the lifestyle we agree with and well, are pretty
much just like us.
But, they are people who probably already know you.
How do we bring unbelievers to you if we can't show
them your love?
Do we get in the way of your work instead of helping?
God, open our eyes to our own sins.
Break our hearts for breaking yours.
God, challenge us to get serious about facing, confessing
and asking your victory from our own sin.
Father, give us compassionate hearts to understand
the pain and suffering of others for all people do
have pain.
Help us, Father, to love like Jesus loved and to leave
everything else to you.

Give your burdens to the LORD,
and he will take care of you.
He will not permit the godly
to slip and fall.

Psalm 55:22

Broken Heart

Death. It hurts so much. When someone you love dies, it leaves a gaping wound in your heart, your world, your days. Grief can be consuming. Sometimes losing a loved one is hard to understand because their death seems so senseless. And, yes, sometimes it is. Perhaps you faced an illness of a loved one and prayed with all your heart, begging God for complete healing of this one who means so much to you. You offered those prayers in faith; believing that God would hear and act.

But when your loved one died, what could you do with your pain?

The only thing you can do is give it to God. There's no other way to deal with it that can bring you peace and heart health. What can you expect from him? Comfort. Peace. Strength to get through the pain. He cares about your grief. He does. He cares. He gets it. He understands the pain; the loneliness; the confusion; the loss. He will get you through it if you will let him. When you hurt, tell him. When you think you can't go on, turn to him. Let him take care of you.

My heart is broken, God.

Not just cliché broken. It's bruised and wounded.

I thought you would heal him. I believed you would.

He's gone too soon, too young.

Do you know how I will miss him?

O God, I need you.

Comfort my wounded heart.

Give me the strength to get up each day and engage in life.

Help me see hope beyond the darkness of pain.

Don't let this grief bury me, God.

I need you more this day than I ever have before.

Help me to believe that you didn't turn away from my prayer.

Help me see that death is a part of life.

Convince my heart that I will see my loved one again one day because of your promise of Resurrection.

I know that's true. I don't really doubt it.

But I need your strength and love to get through this.

One day at a time.

Then eventually, I will feel the warmth of the sun.

I will appreciate the scent of flowers.

I will smile at the giggle of a child.

I will be OK.

Because of you.

Because you care.

Thank you for your care.

Broken Heart

Moses' arms soon became so tired he could
no longer hold them up. So Aaron and Hur found
a stone for him to sit on. Then they stood
on each side of Moses, holding up his hands.
So his hands held steady until sunset.

Exodus 17:12

Help One Another

Do you allow people to help you when you need it? Or, do you try to keep others from knowing when you're struggling? When someone shows concern for you do you deflect that concern right back at them with questions about how they're doing? Why? Are you just too proud to admit when you need help? Did you know that if you don't let folks help you, you're missing out on something? Letting people into your world enough to encourage you through crises, challenge you to obey God, serve more humbly, love more sincerely. Yes, it's hard to be vulnerable. But, when a friend comes alongside you to help, as Aaron and Hur did for Moses, great things can happen.

God created us to live together by helping one another and caring for one another. If you don't let people do that with you, you cheat them as well as yourself. Be vulnerable enough to let others help you and be willing enough to help someone else. The blessings of community will be far greater than the scariness of being vulnerable.

It's hard to be vulnerable, God.
I think I might be afraid to let someone see the
"Real" me because what if they leave?
What if they see what I struggle with or what I
think and then they just ... leave.
I'd feel exposed and, well, like I must not have been
good enough.

I'm OK with being the one who helps others.
I'm even happy to do that
But letting someone else know my struggles and
needs? Not so much.

I know you made us to live in community.
I get that.
But I am most comfortable keeping my community
on a light, fun ... shallow level.
Am I cheating myself by doing that?
Am I cheating others?
Am I cheating you?

God, show me how to let go of my inhibitions
Regarding letting others know me.
A step at a time. I know it's not going to happen all
at once.
But, I want to know the blessing of knowing others
and being known by them.
Show me how. Help me do it.

Help One Another

Keep away from anything that might
take God's place in your hearts.

1 John 5:21

Guard Your Heart

"You have to be kidding! Something take God's place in my heart? That will never happen." That may be what you say to yourself, and even to God, because you're serious about obeying him. You would not intentionally allow something to become more important to you than God.

But how do you feel when God doesn't answer prayer the way you want him to? How do you feel when a situation you've prayed for continues to worsen? Do you worry over it? Do you challenge God regarding what you perceive to be his lack of action?

Consider this ... you've just allowed yourself to become more important than God because you've shown a lack of trust in him. This may be the most common thing that pushes God out of his rightful, most important position.

Satan knows that there are situations and people you care about. Satan will nudge your heart, constantly telling you that God isn't dealing with them. He will tempt you to pick them back up and in doing so, displace God from his rightful place in your heart.

Don't do it. Don't give in. Trust God's love. Trust his plans. Just trust.

Guard Your Heart

God, never will anything be more important to me than
You are. Never.
Well, I say "never" but then I think about what a worrier
I am.
I pray and pray about things – my kids for instance
And when things don't happen the way I want them to –
I worry. I nag. I beg.
I do everything except ... trust.

The truth is that by my reactions, I am judging you
and declaring you incapable.
And in doing that I am arrogantly putting myself
in your rightful place as my Lord.

Please forgive me, Father.
Help me to truly believe your love
For me
For ones I love.

Help me remember that we must live with the choices
we make.
You won't always interfere to change the results of our
choices so we must live with those results
But you will take the messes we make and turn them to
good.
You'll make lemonade from lemons.
You never walk away, hands tossed up in frustration
Because you love us.
You care.
You turn things meant for evil to good.

Even when I walk through the darkest valley,
I will not be afraid, for you are
close beside me. Your rod
and your staff protect
and comfort me.

Psalm 23:4

Fear

The phone rings. It's the doctor's office ... the call you've been dreading. You hear the word that strikes fear in your heart. "Cancer;" or "there's nothing more we can do" or something equally serious. You suddenly face your own mortality. You knew it was coming and, of course, it will come to all of us someday in one way or another.

What will your response be? Fear? Resignation? Beg God to change the report? There is little doubt that your life will have dark valleys in it. Have you thought about the fact that those valleys become the evidence of whether or not you truly trust God? Really trust him.

A relationship with God that goes deeper than the surface leads to finding comfort and strength from his presence, no matter what trouble comes. His promise to always be present gives an anchor to hold onto. Don't get discouraged, though — a life of faith is a journey so it could take some time to reach that peace; but if you keep turning to him, it will come.

I'm scared, God. I hate to admit it but I'm really scared.
I guess that sort of sounds like I don't trust you.
It's not that I'm afraid of dying. I'm not.
But I am nervous about pain.
I am nervous for my loved ones.
I don't want them to hurt.

Of course I know that no one gets out of this life alive.
I just never thought I'd be facing my mortality ... now.

I need you, God.
I need your strength.
Your comfort.
Your courage.
I need to know, to sense, to be sure of your presence
Right beside me.
Helping me through this.

God, I pray that whatever the outcome of this is,
I pray that I will grow closer to you.
I pray that I will know your presence and love in a way
that I've never experienced before ... with certainty.

I think ... I know ... that will mean more to me than
health or wellness.
I know you love me.
I know you want to be close to me.
I need you like I never have before.

Fear

A gentle answer deflects anger,
but harsh words make tempers flare.

Proverbs 15:1

Staying Cool

Staying cool when someone is blasting fiery words at you can be a challenge. The truth is that some people know how to push your buttons – share in the very ones that will make you crazy and they are quite willing to push them as often as possible. This verse is about reacting calmly, instead of in anger. But what about when someone verbally attacks or hurts someone you love? Yep, staying cool is still the best way to respond. Let's be honest though – sometimes it isn't easy.

While God says "stay cool" and "be gentle" he sometimes also makes you want to protect yourself and those you love. Sometimes you want to claim justice, especially on behalf of those you love. It can be very hard to balance those two things. You don't want to end up being a "doormat" for someone who feels free to attack and complain at will. So what do you do? Only one thing to do ... ask God's help. Ask him to help you say what needs to be said, but to do so gently and calmly, not in anger. Your anger will only feed more anger. Your calmness will stop the feeding frenzy.

Selfishness.
Unkindness.
Cheating.
Lying.
How can people treat others so poorly?
Sometimes I feel like I'm wound too tightly ...
Ready to blow just because I don't understand how people
can be so unkind.

Here's the deal ... we're all in this life together, right?
We only get one trip on this rolling globe.
Why not join together to make it as good as possible?

Some don't though or can't. Number One is all that matters
to them.
They have no kindness, encouragement or support for
anyone else.

God, the gentle answer is so hard when
I see people being unkind or unfair to me or to others.
I want to push their Number One aside to make room for
others.
A gentle answer will take so long to change things!
I want to scream about the injustice!
But then I remember your words. "Be gentle."
I hear you say that I'll get farther with sugar than vinegar.

Help me be the one to stop the anger.
To be kind even when others are not.
To show your love even to those who don't show it back.
Yes, that's the kind of woman I want to be.
I'm going to need your help though – this is bigger than me.

Staying Cool

"I know the plans I have for you,"
says the LORD. "They are plans
for good and not for disaster,
to give you a future and a hope."

Jeremiah 29:11

He's Got Your Back

Maybe you've said, "If only I hadn't done that ... made that choice ... said those words – then this wouldn't have happened." That makes it seem like life's events are an accident. Or that the living is like a row of dominoes that you work for hours to set up, then one false move starts them tumbling until they are all down.

Scripture tells us that God plans out the events of our lives, long before any of us are even a twinkle in our parents' eyes. He knows what choices we'll make. He knows what words we will speak and he knows what the outcome of all those will be. Do you know what that means? God has your back. No matter how badly you think you've screwed up, he has a "next." He can make lemonade from the lemons of life.

So what are you going to do with that realization? Only one thing to do, right? Thank him for taking your bad decisions and turning them to good. Praise him for not giving up on you. Honor him because he loves you more than you can ever imagine and yes ... he's got your back!

He's Got Your Back

I just want to say thank you.
Thank you for taking the messes I make and turning
them to good.
O God, I don't set out to make bad choices.
I don't intentionally disobey (at least most of the
time I don't).
I don't rebelliously insist on my own way ...
Well, sometimes I do.

When my choices have backed me up against a
100-foot-tall brick wall.
I have no idea how you can make something good
out of my life this time.
But you do. You always do.
I wonder if sometimes you shake your head at me
or maybe you laugh at my lack of vision (wonder if
God actually laughs?)

I'm so thankful that you do not give up on me.
Thank you for seeing my heart
That it longs to obey
That it is learning how to do this journey with you.
Somehow you take every challenge I give you and
redirect it to something positive and beautiful and then
I have another chance to learn
To serve
To love.

It's amazing that you have a plan for me
And even with the twists and turns that I take
you will accomplish that plan.
Because you love me.
You've got my back.
Amazing.

If someone has enough money to live
well and sees a brother or sister
in need but shows no compassion - how
can God's love be in that person?

1 John 3:17

God's Love in Us

The challenge in this verse seems so simple, doesn't it? If you have more than you need, share with those who don't have enough. Got it. We're done here. Only, we're not because there are still people around the world who are hungry, thirsty, naked, homeless and hopeless. Well, how can that be? If we who "have enough" and claim to be Jesus-followers are truly following the instructions in this verse, then we would be showing God's love through sharing and giving. Is it that there are too many of "them" and not enough of "us"? Maybe.

But maybe it is that we keep too much of our living well money so that we still live well while others can barely live at all. Maybe we aren't willing to give sacrificially, in a way that makes our lifestyle much more simple. This is a challenge each of us must face personally and decide in his or her own heart how to live and give. But ... maybe it's something we each need to think about. Because if we don't think about others' needs, how can God's love be in us? Hmmm.

God's Love in Us

We hear the pleas of children
Who have no homes
Who have no food
Who need clothes and shoes and backpacks.

And we wonder where you are.

We see hurricane-ravaged land
We see destroyed houses
Furniture, toys and precious belongings scattered.
We hear the pain as tired people wonder what to do next.

And we wonder where you are.

We see starving children, ribs sticking out
Bombed out buildings
Towns destroyed
Families broken apart
Peace gone.

And we wonder where you are.

You are ... right here.

You called us – your people – members of the human race
To care for one another
To help one another
To give
To share
So no one is hungry or homeless
To help.

We are here. Your people, O God
Giving, sharing, helping.

If we confess our sins to him,
he is faithful and just to
forgive us our sins and to
cleanse us from all wickedness.

1 John 1:9

The Importance of Confession

Everyone wants forgiveness. Yep, many of us grate-
fully thank God for his generous forgiveness of our
many shortcomings and failures. We say amen and
go right on with our lives. But there's an important
part of this promise of forgiveness that's easy to skip
over – confession.

Ouch. Now, there is little doubt that it's sometimes
hard to speak our failures out loud. After all, God already knows what our sins are, so why do we need to
tell him? Why can't we just skip over that step and go
right to the good stuff – asking for his forgiveness?
There's at least one pretty important reason. That
is because when we take time to specifically confess
our sins, we recognize those sins. It's hard to justify
something when you've just had to admit to it. Once
we recognize (and confess) our sins, we can ask God's
help in putting those sinful behaviors behind us. We
know what to look for as God provides his strength
and help. When we see his help, we can embrace it
and let him cleanse and strengthen us to become
more like him. We begin working as a team with God!

Voices. Voices that whisper, "You weren't wrong. You should have won. You deserved better. A white lie is OK. Cheating is no big deal."
Voices that let us justify our sins.
Voices that come from within us.
Our voices. Satan's voice. Wrong voices.
Voices so convincing that we ignore the privilege of confession.
Yes, it is a privilege.
It is a privilege to stand before you, Almighty Creator God who made us.
God who sees our hearts.
God who seeks our obedience.
God who teaches right from wrong.
God who offers grace.
God who forgives.
God who cleanses.

Confession is a privilege you have given us, Father.
Confessing – not just to you but also to ourselves.
We have the privilege of facing our sins head on
Confessing, repenting and then
Through your grace, O God
Receiving forgiveness and
being made clean.
Clean. Fresh start. New chance.
Thank you for forgiveness.

The Importance
of Confession

Stay alert! Watch out for your great enemy,
the devil. He prowls around like a
roaring lion, looking for
someone to devour.

1 Peter 5:8

Pay Attention!

You don't really hear much about the devil these days. We just don't talk about him often. Maybe we feel that if we don't talk about him then he isn't actually busy bothering us. Sort of "out of sight, out of mind." If only.

Peter knew. He warned his early readers to pay attention. That warning is for us, too. Satan is still our active enemy. An enemy is busy all the time, prowling, searching, waiting for a chance to make his mark.

Do you take him seriously? Do you know he is looking for ways to suck away your faith in God? Think about the places where you are weak – places where you can be tempted to give in to doing what you know you shouldn't. Things like negativity or a critical attitude that seeps into your thoughts all too often. Things like anger, jealousy, shouting at the children, nagging a friend or spouse, doubting God's love or guidance. Whatever your weak spot is, the enemy knows those things and you had better bet they raise their tempting heads often in your days. That's no accident. He's prowling, waiting, wanting to devour. Pay attention!

Pay Attention!

Well, we can't say we haven't been warned.
You warned us. You told us to watch out for the enemy.
He's real. He's not a costume with horns and forked tail
to be worn on Halloween.
He's real ... and constantly on the move looking for ways
to attack and bring us down.

Why don't we take him seriously? We are we so lax?
He becomes like the bad guy in a super hero movie –
Awful, powerful, wicked, evil but ... not actually real.

Wake us up, God! Wake us up to his reality. Wake us up to
the ways he picks and nitpicks on us; pulling us down at
our weak points.
Wake us up to his prowling. He's watching and waiting
for when he can sneak into our thoughts, words, actions.

We need your Holy Spirit, Lord.
We need your protection.
We need your wisdom.
We need to name him ... Satan.
We need your awareness to see him lurking in the
darkness.
We need your help in recognizing his evil,
tempting whisper.

Wake us up, God. Call us to attention.
Arm us with your armor and shield.

We need your help with this. We really do.

Don't look out only for your own interests,
but take an interest in others, too.

Philippians 2:4

It's Not All about You

News flash! Life is not all about you. Sorry, my friend but there's a world full of people around you who have problems, needs, pain, joy … just like you. Now, pretty much everything in our world urges you to take care of #1, make sure you get what you deserve (which is pretty much anything that makes you happy), make sure that you're always comfortable, that you have everything you need, that the world is paying attention to you. The trend is definitely to look out for yourself, even if getting what you want causes problems for someone else.

But, none of that is the way God says to live. A woman who is living for God and showing his love to the world does look out for others. She is willing to be a voice for those who have no voice either because they are a minority or they are too weak to be heard. As God's person in the world, put your own interests aside and look out for others. It's what God says to do.

What would the world be like if we (God's people) forgot
about ourselves?
What if we thought about others instead?
Would an amazing, powerful love flow throughout the
world?
A love that overpowers hate and prejudice?
Would those who feel marginalized then feel loved ... that
they matter?
Would we become a voice for those who have no voice ...
Would they feel heard?
Would we all become family ... looking out for each other?

Dear God, wouldn't this love change the world for the
better?
Would wrongs be righted?
Would hearts be made tender?
Would anger be calmed?
Would differences be forgotten?
Would wars stop?

Isn't this what you want? You want us to take care of
each other. You want us to consider others more
important than ourselves.
Show us how. Light a fire in us to care about others
with such passion that we forget ourselves.
A passion that challenges us to right wrongs,
to speak out, to stand up. To make a difference.

Fill us, God, with your love for others
And help us to get ourselves out of the way so that love
can make a difference.

It's Not All
about You

"Give, and you will receive. Your gift
will return to you in full - pressed down,
shaken together to make room for more,
running over, and poured into your lap.
The amount you give will determine
the amount you get back."

Luke 6:38

Brown Sugar

When I was a little girl I loved when my mom baked chocolate chip cookies. Yumm. One of the intriguing ingredients of that recipe is brown sugar. Unlike most dry baking ingredients, which are sifted and gently measured, brown sugar is crammed into the measuring cup. Just when I thought the cup was full, Mom would put in a little more and press it down. Surely it was full then. Nope, she added more and more and more. I couldn't believe how much brown sugar she got into that measuring cup.

God's blessings are like that brown sugar. This verse promises that if we give, we will get back more than we can even imagine. So ... give what? What's this talking about? Give our hearts to God. Give our time, strength and devotion to him. Take care of others by loving, giving our time, strength, energy, money ... whatever is needed. Give till it hurts. Give without thinking about it. Just give. Give out of our love for him and desire to serve him. God's blessings will fill our hearts and lives like brown sugar in a measuring cup. Even more.

God, we sadly are a people who expect.
We expect
The world to treat us kindly
A comfortable home
A soft bed
Good food
Clean water
Safety
Health
Families to love
Friends to laugh with.

We expect
Your blessings
Your gifts
Your love
Your protection ...

Yet so much of what we have we take for granted
Because ...
We expect.

Loving, Giving Father
Open our eyes to your blessings in our lives.
Open our hearts to pay attention
To actually see all you give us each day.

Show us the blessing of suffering because then we
lean on you.
The blessing of pain so we appreciate health.
The blessing of nothing so we appreciate some.
The blessing of loss so we appreciate love.

May our hearts be thankful, O God, for all you give.

Brown Sugar

I am praying to you because I know you will answer,
O God. Bend down and listen as I pray.

Psalm 17:6

Believe It!

Not many things in this world are things you can be certain of. The truth is that sometimes people let you down; even people you love. Situations can change on a moment's notice so you can't plan on things always being what you expect. Jobs are lost. Sickness happens. People leave. Actually the only thing you can be certain of is that things will change.

No wait. There is one thing you can actually be certain of and that is that God will answer your prayers. The psalmist knew that. He believed that God would hear his prayer and answer. That's why he kept praying. He believed he could go to God with anything.

Do you believe that? Do you trust that God hears your prayers – even the simplest ones? Even the ones that are just for you? After all, there are some major things in the world that need his attention. Oh yes, he does hear and he will answer because he loves you. Whatever is on your heart matters to him. He wants to hear every detail and he will answer. Believe it.

Believe It!

You promise and we believe.
We show our belief by prayers of
Praise
Honor
Love
Requests
Fear
Hope.
We know you hear because you said you would.

Our hearts cry out to you and because you hear
We draw closer to you
We know you better.
With each answered prayer
We are changed
By knowing that you care
You have a plan
You hear our concerns.

Even when your answers are not exactly what we want
We learn to believe that you are doing what is best.
We learn the importance
Necessity
Blessing
Of leaning on you in our sorrow and fear.
We learn to trust.
In the end, that's what it's all about
Trusting you.

Fix your thoughts on what is true,
and honorable, and right, and pure,
and lovely, and admirable. Think
about things that are excellent
and worthy of praise.

Philippians 4:8

What You Put in Is What Comes Out

Be careful what you put into your mind. Now, you may think, "Hey, I'm a serious follower of Jesus, so why do I need this reminder?" Consider that it may be in Scripture because God knows that it's easy for us to get lazy once in a while. Think about it – when life gets crazy busy, isn't it easy to get lax about what movies or TV shows you watch, what stories you listen to, what things grab your attention online? You try to relate to folks so that you can be a witness of God's love but then it's tempting to get into conversations that are not honoring to God or other people. The whole "true, honorable, right, pure, lovely and admirable" thing goes right out the window.

The trouble is that what you put "in" will eventually come "out." So if you repeatedly put unkind, unclean, self-centered, unloving things into your mind they will affect the way you treat others. It's virtually impossible to put those things in your mind and still reflect God's love to those around you and that's what matters, right? Being God's woman to share his love with those around you. Be careful what you put in.

What You Put in
Is What Comes Out

It's a struggle to walk the line between obedience to you
and relating to the people I'm around every day.
I don't want to be weird – or "holier than thou."
I just want to show my devotion to you.

Stuff sneaks in so quietly I sometimes don't notice.
Stuff I don't really want to say or do. It just happens.
I guess that's the devil's sneakiness.

Help me, Father, to remember what I'm about.
And to call on you to guard
My eyes
My ears
My thoughts
My words.
Help me shut down tempting situations.
Give me courage to gently walk away when I must.
Remind me that every word and action reflects to
others what I really think of you.

Wow. That truth scares me
Because I want the world to know that I love you.
I want to honor and obey you.
I want others to know your love.
I don't want to be a roadblock to that happening.

I can't do this by myself.
I need your Spirit to help me guard what I allow in
my heart so that you can control what words and
actions come out of me.
That's what I want.

My health may fail, and my spirit may
grow weak, but God remains the
strength of my heart;
he is mine forever.

Psalm 73:26

Strength

Life is full of bumps. There's no getting around that. Sometimes the problems that roll through our lives are just speed bumps – irritating and annoying but not really biggies. Sometimes those problems are crises that become brick walls. We have to wait to see how God will lead us around them or over them. Sometimes he even knocks them down. It takes patience. (Great, who is really good at patience?)

No one enjoys problems. However, it is in problems that we learn and grow because that's when our trust in God becomes real – even to us. There is a choice to make when life starts to crumble. Do you choose to stick with God? To trust him, no matter what? You will need patience to see what God is going to do. But, making the choice to trust him, then waiting for his guidance and work, gives you opportunity to see his love and care for you. Of course, the Evil One will do all he can to discourage you and pull you away from your choice to trust God. Don't listen to him. Don't give up. Choose God and be strong in holding to that choice.

Strength

Why does the Evil One have so much success in my life?
I think I've made my choice to stick with you, God, to
trust you no matter what, but then ...
Before I know it, I begin to feel like I'm suffering and
you're not paying attention.
The Evil One quietly suggests that you must be busy
with things that are more important to you and that my
measly problems are ... measly.
Then my choice to stick with you is on quicksand and I
can barely lift one foot to put in front of the other.
I sink into the pit of feeling ignored, unloved,
unimportant ... defeated.
And the Evil One has won.

Still ... in my heart I know that you really do love me.
I know you do have a plan.
I need only to trust.
To be patient and trust.
Yeah, that patience thing doesn't come so easily.

I need your help to ...
Push aside the nagging thoughts the Evil One sends
To believe
To trust
To persevere
To choose YOU and to be strong in holding to that choice.
No matter what.

Trust in the LORD with all your heart;
do not depend on your own understanding.
Seek his will in all you do, and he will
show you which path to take.

Proverbs 3:5-6

Control Issues

Life needs a "Resign" button. OK, maybe not totally resign but an "I'm sorry Mom/Wife/Grandma/Friend/Volunteer is not in today. Please leave a brief message and I'll get back to you when I can handle life again. Oh, and ... don't hold your breath."

Maybe it feels that life is too much because women are nurturers and caregivers. But have you ever over-cared? The definition of that is when you care so much that you can't let go of a situation. It keeps you up at night. It causes you to pig out on junk (comfort) food. It consumes your thoughts and prayers. Perhaps it's when you're there that you start looking for that "out of the office today" button.

The real issue may not be over-care. It may be control. Who is in control? Do you think it's you? Silly you. Do you really get to tell others what's best for them, what decisions to make and even better than that, do you get to tell God what to do? Yeah, how's that going for you?

The more people you care about, the more consuming life can be. But a "Put life on hold" button isn't the answer. Submitting to God is. Give up control. God can handle all the stuff. He can't over-care because he cares totally. Let God be God.

Why?
Why do I continually try to run others' lives?
Why do I stress over their choices and what the long-term
consequences might be?
Why? Because letting go scares me.

God, do you know how scary letting go feels?
What if bad things happen to people I care about?
What if I could have stopped those bad things?

The thing is that in my gut I know I can't stop them.
Only you can help, protect and guide them.
Why can't I just trust you to take care of them?
I say I do. But I don't.
Too many of my prayers are filled with instructions for you –
Just so you know what to do.

My desire is to let you be you. Let God be God.
My life would be a lot less stressful, wouldn't it?
And truth is that I'm not making a single change in any
outcome by my stressing and instruction-giving.

Trust. That's what I need. To trust you, God. To believe
that you will take care of things from the depths of your
unbelievable love for me and those I love.

I want to trust your love. So today I will choose that trust.
I know I will need to choose it over and over and over until
it sticks and that's the first place I go.
Control issues submitted to amazing love beginning now.

Control Issues

"Be still, and know that I am God!"

Psalm 46:10

Just Stop!

The act of being still does not happen very often in our multitask-oriented world. We're so busy that it's unusual to even be doing only one thing at a time. There are those few moments before we fall asleep at night, in the silence of a darkened room, but how often do we fall asleep to our minds forming lists and reminders of tomorrow's tasks?

Is it possible that God's command to be still is one of the most difficult to obey in our world today? We're so busy. We're so task oriented. We want to be the best moms, offering our children every opportunity to experience life at its fullest. We want to be supportive wives. We want to be successful employees, friends, neighbors and volunteers. In short, we fill our lives so full that there isn't much time left to be still.

What are we missing? Time to focus on God's love and allowing it to bring peace to our hearts. A reminder of God's strength and power. Guidance through his Holy Spirit speaking into our hearts. If we don't get still and focus on God, we will miss the opportunity to know his love more deeply. So, just stop. Be still. Know love.

Just Stop!

Noise. Commitments. Work. Children. Friends. Parents.
My life is filled with people and stuff.
I seriously wonder if I'm losing my mind when my
thoughts are bombarded with "Do this next. This is
more important. You should ... You must ..."
I can't take it anymore, God.
I miss quiet.
I miss solitude.
I miss peace.
I miss ... you.

Your simple call to "Be still" is hard to come by in this
world of high achievements and unreal standards of
excellence.

Our "connected every moment" world tells us what a
creative mom, loving wife, high-achieving employee and
even what a dedicated believer looks like.
It's too much. Too much.
I can't do it all. In fact I can't do any of it and still find
the time to be still ... without falling asleep.

God, help me know when to say ENOUGH.
No more social media input.
No more well-meaning words from good Christian writers
and speakers.
No more busyness.

Help me, loving Father, to stop. To be still.
Just be quiet with you so that I can
Know your love
Sense your power
Hear your guidance
Be yours.

Share each other's burdens,
and in this way obey the law of Christ.

Galatians 6:2

Living in Community

We're in this life together. We are to walk alongside one another; helping, encouraging, celebrating life and all it brings.

It's a good plan. God knew that we're better with others than we are alone. Hard times are more bearable when they are shared with those who care. Strength in scary times grows deeper through caring friends sharing their strength. Celebrations are a lot more joyous when others cheer with you. We're just better when we share life with others.

When you think about it, there are two elements to this command. One is to compassionately invest in others' lives. Share their burdens. Really share – invest by caring, spending time, listening. It's good to pray for others, but sharing can be done on a much deeper level and God seems to be suggesting that deeper sort of caring.

There is a second part of this and in some ways it may be more difficult. That is to allow others into your life. Burdens cannot be shared if you aren't willing to let others into the good, bad and ugly of your life. The simple message of this verse is God bringing us into community with others – sharing in one another's lives. It's his plan.

Living in
Community

You made us to live in community
To help and encourage each other.
That's good. It's hard to navigate this life alone.

But, the thing is … well, it's hard sometimes.
Hard to let others see when I'm struggling.
I'm afraid my struggles make me look weak or worse
than that … unspiritual. God forbid.
No, I can't be that vulnerable.
I don't want to need anyone.
I want to "appear" to have life well in control.

Of course, I don't mind being there for others who
need help.
After all, that's what you told us to do – help others so,
yeah, I do want to do that.

But unfortunately … no fortunately but not easily
I see that the suggestion to share each other's burdens
is not a suggestion, but a command and that it applies
to both sides – helping others and … letting others
help me.

I need your Spirit's help to let down my guard and
give others a chance to be needed. That's what builds
community, isn't it?
So …
Help me learn to be open.
Help me learn to be vulnerable.
Help me learn to let others help me.

Help me allow others to serve you by serving me.

Jesus said, "Come to me, all of you who
are weary and carry heavy burdens,
and I will give you rest."

Matthew 11:28

A Lot of Love

Jesus loves you very much. He wants you to know that. His love is so large that it's sometimes hard to wrap your mind around its greatness. How can a perfect being love someone who is so inconsistent and who messes up so often? How can the God of creation, who has so much to take care of in this troubled world, actually have time to think about you? Well, he does.

Do you need a reminder of how much he loves you? Think about these words of Jesus. He said, "Come." Just come to him. He's inviting you. He wants you to come. He knows you're tired. He knows that life weighs heavy sometimes. He not only understands all of that, he cares about it. That's why he invites you to come to him and bring all your cares. Then he promises to give you rest. Rest. What a beautiful word. This isn't just "sit down and take a load off" rest. It isn't just eight hours of uninterrupted sleep. It's better than that. It's "I will take those burdens off your heart and mind. I will handle them so that you CAN rest." There's a lot of love in that simple offer to come to him and receive rest. A lot of love.

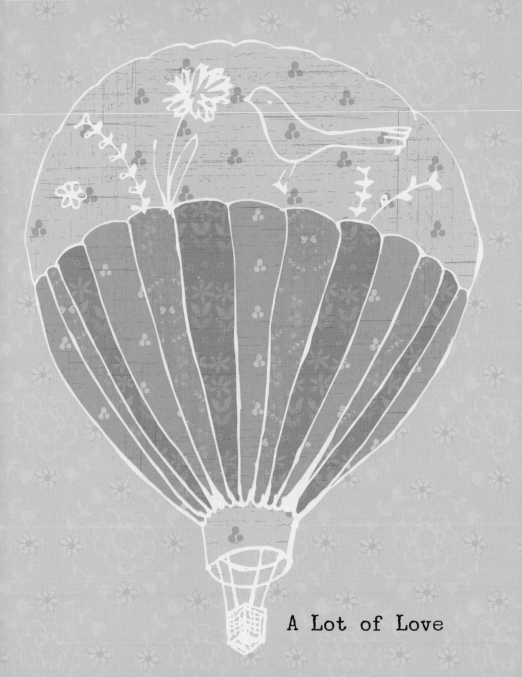

A Lot of Love

My loving God,
Your invitation to bring you my burdens is what I need.
It's what I want ... but it apparently is not a "one and
done" kind of thing.
I try to give them to you but it's hard to leave them alone.
When the stress kicks in at those panic-filled 2 AM
wake-ups I grab them right back.

My Father, help me to receive and accept your offer of rest.
Remind me through the power of your Spirit in my heart
that you care; you are working; you've got things
under control.

Remind me, Father, of all the ways you have already
shown your love in my life.
Remind me, Father, that you know all that has happened,
is happening, and will happen.

In that reminding, Father, stop me from taking my burdens
back.
When I come to touch them, handle them, pick at them,
remind me anew that you are working.

Help me to rest ... to take a breath and release my
stress in a deep sigh of relief that I can trust you.

Thank you for your love that offers this rest.
I can't comprehend it.
I want it.
I'm so thankful for it.

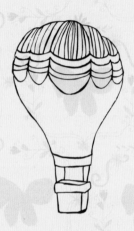

Create in me a clean heart,
O God. Renew a loyal spirit within me.

Psalm 51:10

Start Fresh

"It's not over 'til it's over." That's the wonderful thing about life with God. Here's the pattern that happens way too often: You commit to follow him, obey him, serve him and, yes, you start strong. But time after time you mess up by insisting on your own way, fighting for control, refusing to love other people ... well, there are just so very many ways to break that commitment. Everyone does. We simply can't help it.

The beauty of a relationship with God is that those commitment breaks do not mark the end of the relationship. God loves you so much and he waits for you to come back to him. That's what this psalmist's prayer is all about – asking God to clean up your heart and help you start fresh on the path of obedience and service. Of course, God does his part and answers this prayer. You learn something (hopefully) each time you falter in your walk with him. The best thing you learn may be that he is right there waiting for you to come back and start fresh again. He loves you that much.

Start Fresh

O God, how many times am I going to need "do-overs"?
I'm so frustrated. I try. I really do but then
I get so filled up with ... me.
I don't mean to, Father.
I can't even explain how it happens.
I want to serve you.
I want to reflect your love.
I long that people will feel they've spent time with a
Jesus-follower when they spend time with me.
I long for that.
But I get so caught up in ... me.

Thank you for not giving up on me regardless of how
many fresh starts I need.
Thank you for teaching me something new each time I
need a fresh start.
Thank you for cleaning my heart that gets so filthy with
Selfishness
Ego
Pride
And a million other sins.

Thank you for a fresh start and the opportunity to start
again on the path to knowing and serving you.

God, my heart's desire is to be your woman in the world
where you have placed me.
Help me to be more true to you this day than I was
yesterday and yes, even more true in every tomorrow.

"If you love only those who love you,
what reward is there for that?
Even corrupt tax collectors do that much."

Matthew 5:46

Loving Others

Let's be honest, most people are usually kind and loving and they choose to be – not just because God said to be. They love because they want to be kind and supportive to others. Well, most others. Some others.

Well, the more diverse and, yes, loose our world becomes, the more some of us confine our love to those who think and behave as we do. Some just find it difficult to separate their disapproval of lifestyles from the individuals living them. Then it's difficult to honestly love those individuals. Love shows, you know. It shows by the words spoken, attitude projected, by the separation into "us vs. them."

It's OK to have beliefs, morals and standards. We are to be "in the world" but not "of the world." And, of course it is wonderful to love your family, friends and Christian brothers and sisters. But God's command to love is bigger than that. We are also to show God's love to those who aren't like us and who may even annoy or anger us. It's kind of hard to be critical and judgmental and also be loving. God says to love others. Not just those who are like us. Love all others.

Loving Others

God, I ask your Holy Spirit to teach me to love.
Teach me to love the ones I don't really want to love.
Because that's the problem, isn't it?
Loving people who frighten me by how they
Speak
Dress
Believe.
I think I know how to love. I mean, how hard can it be?
But when I'm honest I must admit that there are those I
do not actually love.
Instead I turn my eyes away from those who make me
uncomfortable ...
Perhaps those who most need to know of your love.

Father, I don't want to have an "us vs. them" mentality.
You don't. You love all.
Open my eyes to see the hearts of those who are
different from me.
Help me to see the loneliness or fear or insecurity or
whatever they may be feeling. Help me to see that they
aren't so different from me after all.

Love through me.
Speak through me.
Use me as your voice, hands, feet ... heart
To show your love to others and in the process
Learn to love them myself.

Then Jesus wept.

John 11:35

Eternal Promises

If a person ever needed proof that Jesus cares, here it is. Jesus cried. God cried. Wow. But what's important to note here is not just that Jesus wept but why he wept. He didn't weep just because his friend had died. He didn't weep just because Lazarus's sisters were heartbroken. He wept because they just didn't get it. How many times had he taught them about God's love and the promise of eternity with him? How often had he said that death isn't the end? They seemed to understand. They said they believed. But when the rubber met the road, their emotions, grief and fear took over. So Jesus wept a little from his sorrow that his friends were hurting but also from sorrow that they still didn't deeply believe.

Where are you on the belief scale? You believe that you believe. But when loss comes or the anxious anticipation of loss, how do you handle it? Are you able to grab on to the promise of resurrection and hold on tight? Does that promise, wrapped in God's love, walk you through your anxiety, fear and grief? It's hard. No doubt about it. But, at the end of the fear and grief, hopefully you can grab on to his promises that are filled with love and hope for an eternity together with him and those you love.

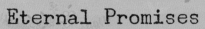

Eternal Promises

How often do I break your heart by my self-centered
unbelief?
Oh, I say the right words.
I even think I believe.
But when life gets tough I see just how deep my belief
doesn't go.

The truth, however, is that I'm tired.
I'm tired of not believing.
I'm tired of worrying.
I'm tired of grieving.

I long to believe your promises.
I long to trust your heart.
I long to learn and grow and go deeper and deeper in
my walk with you.

Help me, Father, to let go of my unbelief
Because, yes, I hold on to it by fighting to have control
of my life.
I hold on to it by fear.
I hold on to it by not trusting your heart and your love.

It breaks my heart to think that I hurt you by my
unbelief.
You've done so much to clearly show your love
and care.
You've given everything.

Open my eyes to your love.
Loosen my grip on me
Deepen my trust in you.

"I hold you by your right hand - I,
the LORD your God. And I say to you,
'Don't be afraid. I am here to help you.'"

Isaiah 41:13

Feeling Safe

Remember the security that you felt as a child when Mom or Dad would take your hand to guide you across a busy street or to keep you close in a crowded place? You knew you were loved and cared for. You knew that your parent would protect you no matter what. There was nothing to be afraid of. What a wonderful feeling of security.

Who holds your hand now when life gets dangerous or scary? If you have put your trust in God, he does. He promises security that is even deeper than that childhood safety and love you recall. Regardless of what you're going through — scary situations with unknown outcomes; new experiences that make you feel insecure; heart-ripping grief; or just regular, every day life ... he's holding your hand. He said he would. Even when life gets messy and hard, he wants the comfort of his hand holding yours to give you courage. He loves you. He doesn't want you to be afraid. Be still and visualize his hand holding yours. Feel the warmth of your loving Father's hand wrapped around yours. Let your heart find comfort and peace.

Feeling Safe

Safety. That's what we all really want, isn't it?
I want to know that whatever happens, I will be safe.
Storms.
Earthquakes.
Fires.
Broken relationships.
Illness.
Death.

Will I be safe from these?

The thing is, I want safety by my own definition.
I want to be completely protected from those things.
I don't want to have to deal with any of that stuff.
That isn't realistic though, is it?
I will have to deal with some of them at least.

What I need to understand is that sometimes my safety
is simply that you are holding my hand.
You are walking with me through the dark times.
Even though I sometimes can't see where my next step
will take me,
I am not alone because you aren't even an arm's length
away.

You did not promise to protect me from the storms but
you did promise to walk with me through them.
Nothing that happens surprises you.
If I can learn to trust you my faith in you will grow
deeper and more meaningful.

So, thank you for your presence.
Thank you for holding my hand.
Thank you for your love.
Thank you for getting me through the storms.

Among all the parts of the body, the tongue is
a flame of fire. It is a whole world of
wickedness, corrupting your entire body.
It can set your whole life on fire,
for it is set on fire by hell itself.

James 3:6

Sticks and Stones

The old adage, "Sticks and stones may break my bones but words will never hurt me" is simply not true. Words have so very much power. Critical, hurtful words spoken toward another will lie like a weight on his or her spirit. Even if the one who spoke the words apologizes, their power is not erased because somehow critical, hurtful words often speak into our own insecurities — the negative things we believe to be true about ourselves. They feed an already weak self-image. Actually, in this social media-oriented world, words do not have to be spoken. They can be written and broadcast to a large audience. Then the writer can feel somewhat anonymous and the attack feels less personal. But it isn't. The damage is still done to the heart and spirit of the object of the words.

The dilemma comes when you claim to follow Christ and share his love with others but your words (written or spoken) are unkind and hurtful. You can't have it both ways. Even if you feel your words are justified because they describe a lifestyle or behavior that goes against Scripture you must be careful that your actual words or even the tone of your words do not adversely affect your witness as a child of God. Watch your words. They make a difference.

Sticks and Stones

Words. My words.
To be honest, I seldom think about the damage they can do
to another's soul.

I spit out words in anger or frustration. Hurling them at
another or about another (behind her back of course).
When I'm angry, I don't really care who hears my words.

Or sometimes I frame my words just to make someone
laugh.
It feels good to entertain a friend. But how often are my
humorous words – funny only for the moment –
spoken at the expense of another?

Dear God, forgive my careless words.
Words that damage and sting.
Words that leave a scar, even if I never meant them in the
first place.

Forgive my words of anger.
Words that spring from selfishness and pride.
Words that hurt others.
Others, who do not deserve to be the victims of my words.

I ask you, Father, to stop my hurtful words.
Stop me from speaking, writing, even thinking them.
Remind me to measure my words.
Fill my lips ... my thoughts with helpful, encouraging,
loving words.
Words that will help another person be better, stronger,
and more sure of my love and concern and your love and
concern.

Remind me of the power of words. My words.

We are God's masterpiece. He has created
us anew in Christ Jesus, so we can
do the good things he planned
for us long ago.

Ephesians 2:10

God's Masterpiece

A masterpiece is considered the best work of an artist ... usually his very best work. This is often the work that the artist is best known for. It might even become synonymous with the artist's name. Knowing that, how does it make you feel to know that YOU are God's masterpiece? Think about all the amazing things God created – from the most beautiful and amazing natural things on our planet to the most intricate delicate creature, his creativity is beyond comprehension. He has made some pretty amazing things ... but YOU are his masterpiece.

God spent six days creating our beautiful world and everything in it. But he saved the best for last when he made people in his own image. People can think, make decisions, love, care for others, be productive. We are complex and intelligent. He loves us so much that he sent his son to die for our sins.

So, do you choose to live like a masterpiece? Are you convinced of your worth and value in God's eyes or do you feel like a mass reproduced fake piece of art? You do have value – you are his masterpiece! Choose to live in that truth.

God's Masterpiece

I am your masterpiece? Really? Me?
Seriously God, have you noticed how often I fail?
The promises I make ... and break?
The daily resolutions to trust and obey yet the worry
and stress that fill my heart and thoughts?
Knowing the command to love but my actions are filled
with selfishness?

O God, I try to live for you. Try to obey you. Try to
serve you
But I fail ... over and over.

The only reason I can be called your masterpiece is
Because of
Your love
Your grace
Your forgiveness.

You know all about me.
My thoughts
My selfishness
My sin
And yet you not only love me
You have a plan for me
You want to grow my faith in you
You have tasks for me that lets me partner in your work
You love me and will bring me into your eternity.

God, let this realization change me.
Make me more diligent in serving
More intentional in living
More hungry to know and grow and love.
Keep me on a path of being worthy of being called your
masterpiece.

The LORD is my strength and shield.
I trust him with all my heart.
He helps me, and my heart is filled
with joy. I burst out in songs
of thanksgiving.

Psalm 28:7

Spontaneous Joy

Perhaps you have witnessed ear-numbing outbursts of joy and excitement at sporting events or concerts. When their team scores or makes an awesome play, fans cannot control their excitement so it explodes in cheers and jumping about. Or when a favorite musician plays the first chords of a well-loved song, cheers ring through the air and small lights or flames are waved back and forth in time to the music. Unabashed, spontaneous joy is a fun thing to share with other people. It's freeing and uplifting.

So, why are we somewhat reticent to show unabashed, joyful thanksgiving to God? There are "acceptable" ways to show him our thankfulness. We gently lift hands in the air while singing a worship song or we pray heartfelt thanks and those are good things. But we are not likely to spontaneously cheer God with a loud shout and a fist pump. Of course, it's not necessary to bring our appreciation of his work to the level of the expressions of joy for a sporting event, but wouldn't it be fun to let go and just cheer him ... to just shout thanks for his help and strength? Perhaps you do that. If so ... do it more. Explode in thanksgiving for all God does for you and for all he is!

Spontaneous Joy

Ocean waves call out your power.
Towering mountains shout your strength.
Wind blowing through the trees whispers your name.
Birds singing their songs sing of you.

Rivers and oceans
Mountains and valleys
Birds and fish
Stones and trees
All of creation sings your praises, O God.

I join in, O God.
I lift my voice in joy
I raise my hands in praise
I bow my knees in worship.
You are my God
Most awesome
Most loving.

You guide me with your wisdom
You forgive my sins
You bless my days
You give peace to my nights.
You love me through all life
There is none like you.

I will praise you with every breath
I will praise you with energy
I will praise you with joy
I will praise you until the whole world knows.

I pray that God, the source of hope, will fill
you completely with joy and peace because
you trust in him. Then you will overflow
with confident hope through the power
of the Holy Spirit.

Romans 15:13

Hope for Better Times

Sometimes even the brightest sunshiny day is over-shadowed with darkness and a sense of gloom. It's hard to see through the muck of life and to find any reason to have hope for things to get better. That's a hard place to be. It's a scary place to be.

Praying friends are a real gift when you're in a dark pit. Praying for your hope to be in God. Praying for you to see his hand working, however slowly, to bring you back to joy and to give you a sense of peace. Praying for you to place your trust fully, completely, only in him because that is the only place where hope can be found.

So if you have friends praying for you, thank them. Then be open to God's Spirit working in your heart. Be thankful for those glimpses of his work that give you hope for a better future. And, if you have friends going through a difficult time, lift them up to God in prayer. Pray for him to fill them with hope through the power of his Spirit.

Be the recipient or be the giver ... we're all in this life together.

Hope for
Better Times

Thank you for my praying friends
Who bring my name before you often
Asking for your strength to fill me
For hope in your promises to get me through
For my trust in you to grow
For your perfect plan in my life.

Thank you for hearing their prayers
For answering
For caring.

Don't let their prayers go to waste because of me.
Open my heart to your work in it.
Don't let me fight you as you teach me in the dark times.
I pray that I'll be patient and let your Spirit do its
work in my heart.

God, I lift my friends up to you, too.
The ones going through hard times
The ones who are discouraged
The ones who need to be reminded of your presence.

Love them, God.
Guide them.
Remind them that you are there in their darkest hours
And that you will be there when the sun comes out again.
Thank you for the privilege of bringing them to you.

Thank you for the gift of friends
Thank you for the gift of answered prayer.

"It is not my heavenly Father's will that even
one of these little ones should perish."

Matthew 18:14

Don't Ever Give Up

You pray and pray for a loved one to accept Jesus. You carefully craft your words and tend to your attitude when you're around that person so that she sees God's love through you. But sometimes it seems like the more you pray the farther that loved one gets from knowing God. Why is that? It's easy to get discouraged when you've prayed for someone for years and years. Doesn't God hear your prayers? Doesn't he care that there are people who don't know him? Why does it take so long? Will your loved one ever say "yes" to God?

There's no doubt that God wants everyone to know him. He loves mankind. But he also gave people the freedom to choose him or not choose him. He doesn't force anyone to faith. The responsibility is yours to keep sharing, keep praying and never give up. No one knows when God's Spirit may touch a person's heart in just the way that calls that heart to finally respond, "Yes, I want you, God." So, you keep bringing your loved one's name to God. You keep sharing at every opportunity, in love and faith that your loved one will accept Jesus. You just never know when the "yes" will come.

Don't Ever Give Up

It's hard not to get discouraged.
I have prayed for so long for my friend to know you, God.
I've tried to live a good example of a Christ-follower.
But ... nothing.
It would be easy to give up
But I can't.

Eternity is real.
Hell is real.
Evil is real.
Heaven is real.
God is real and I want my friend to know you and to
know she will have eternity with you.

So God, keep me on my knees, so to speak.
Keep her name in my mind so that I lift her to you each
time I think of her.
Fill me with a renewed urgency to pray for her to know
you.
Remind me that you do love her already even more than
I do.
You want her to know you – but you won't push – it's
her choice.
Help me remember that every prayer, every kind word,
every opportunity is laying more of a foundation and
one day, one amazing, wonderful day, she may say yes
to you.
When that day comes, angels will rejoice and so will I
that my friend knows you!

What good is it, dear brothers and sisters,
if you say you have faith but don't show
it by your actions? Can that kind
of faith save anyone?

James 2:14

Say It and Show It

Some people talk a good show. They know all the right Bible verses to quote and all the Christianese to speak to show how spiritual they are. They can win any argument. They can shoot down anyone's sinful lifestyle. They can talk for days about how God loves and they love and blah, blah, blah.

The problem is that their actions don't match their words — at least the words about loving others the way Jesus said to love. A head-knowledge of Scripture and what's right and wrong will seldom convince another of your love for her. Actions are more likely to do that. So, don't tell someone that you love her with a godly love — show her. Live sacrificially and give your time and energy to help someone who can't repay you in any way. Spend time with people, not just to "save" them, but to love them. Do things to help them, babysit their kids, run errands, clean, just listen. Let your actions show your love. The combination of faith and action is ... real faith.

Say It
and Show It

I can say all the Christian words I want –
The right words make me sound like a God-serving
person –
I can sincerely whisper
"God loves you"
"Just pray about it"
To anyone in need
But if I look the other way
When I see people who are hungry
People who are lonely
Someone who needs to be driven to the doctor
A friend who just needs someone to listen
Then my words are empty.
Words that make me feel good but do not serve God or
others.

Open my eyes, Father, to notice others.
Help me to slow down enough to see opportunities to
put my faith words into action
To give them life.
Help me be willing to invest time
To get dirty
To be uncomfortable
To be useful to you.

Fill me with
Courage to step out of my comfort zone
Compassion to invest time from my own life
Willingness to give my energy – to put elbow grease
to my faith so that it helps others, teaches me, builds
community and serves you.

The LORD says, "I will guide you along
the best pathway for your life.
I will advise you and watch over you."

Psalm 32:8

Which Way to Turn

Life throws a sudden curve and everything changes. You probably know the feeling. Maybe a job is gone. Perhaps it's a relationship that ends. A dear loved one passes away. Change is part of life. But sometimes change causes confusion because you wonder which way to go — is it time for a new job, should you move to a new city, is it time to end a relationship — things like that. Big decisions. It can be hard to know what to do.

Thankfully, God will guide you. He says he will, if you will ask him. So, you ask, "God what do I do here? Where do I go?" Then what? How do you know when he is guiding? Sometimes he guides by taking away options. Sometimes he gives you a strong feeling that you know you can't ignore. Sometimes he brings trusted people into your life who give solid advice. He guides because he loves you and wants good things for your life.

If you need direction, ask him. Then pay attention to the things in your world, look for how God is guiding. Be patient. You'll see his hand and through it sense his love.

Which Way to Turn

152

I'm confused. I see good on all sides and I see bad on all sides.
Sometimes it feels like I'm walking through pea soup-thick fog.
I can't see where I'm going. I'm not sure what to do.
I'm scared to make decisions because I don't know which ones are God-directed and which ones are me-directed.
I don't want to mess up my life.

God, I want to be where you want me to be.
I want to do what you want me to do.
It's just that right at the moment I don't feel certain about any of those things.

I long to sense your Spirit moving in my heart ...
Encouraging me to take one step, then the next even if I can't see a safe place to step.
Let me sense your love soaking into my heart because then I'll know that you are paying attention to me.
Do I want to be happy? Yes, of course.
But what will ultimately make me happy is the certainty that I am in the center of your will, even if it's a more painful place to be than I expected.
Pain can teach me a lot.
I know there will be real peace even in that painful place.
Real peace.
So, guide me, Father.
Move me in the direction you want me to go.
I'll pay attention.
I'll obey.

And we are confident that he hears us whenever
we ask for anything that pleases him. And
since we know he hears us when we make
our requests, we also know that he
will give us what we ask for.

1 John 5:14-15

Getting What You Ask For

God hears your prayers. He said he would and he does. Do you believe that? If you do, then it makes sense that prayer is an important part of your life. Is it? When something happens to you or a loved one or when a big decision is looming, is your first thought to take it to God? After all, this verse says that God will give you whatever you ask for.

Hmmm, maybe your first reaction is, "Hey, he doesn't give me whatever I ask for!" Right, that's because there's something else to consider — relationship. Growing in your relationship with God means getting to know him so well that your heart (read wishes, desires, hopes) becomes more aligned with his. You want his will in your life, no matter what. That simply means that you become more submitted to his will. The relationship is based on trust and the belief that God loves you more than you can even imagine. Because of that you believe that he hears your prayers and will give you the desires of your heart — your heart that is eager to serve and obey him. There's the reason that the first thing you want to do with any situation is take it to God. You know he hears. You know he answers. You know he loves you.

Getting What
You Ask For

O God, of course I come right to you with my concerns.
But I have to confess that my prayer is not usually
one of submission but of instruction.
I pray to tell you exactly how to handle situations –
You know, just in case you need my help.

I'm sorry, Father. I really am.
I know I can talk with you about anything and even
tell you how I would prefer you to handle things.
But as my whispered "amen" dies out I pray for my
Heart to be ready
Willing
Happy
To accept whatever comes.
It may not be easy sometimes. That's OK. You love me.
It may not be the way I would have wanted. That's OK.
You know best.

It is incredible that you listen to my prayers
Even when I ramble
Even when I beg
Even when I nag
You listen. You care. You see a bigger picture and you
will do what is best.
And, as I spend more time with you and understand
this Jesus-life better, my prayers are healthier, wiser
and less selfish.
So we walk together. We work together. And I am
blessed to be the child of my Father who cares so
much.

What do you have that God hasn't given you?
And if everything you have is from God,
why boast as though it were not a gift?

1 Corinthians 4:7

Humility Wins

Pride is a funny thing. Being filled with pride to the point of bragging about yourself or your accomplishments is not a good thing. But you are supposed to take pride in what you do and work to the best of your ability — especially when working for the Lord.

Be cautious of becoming so convinced of the awesomeness of your abilities and talents that you forget who gave them to you. God decided that you should be good at singing, writing, designing, math ... whatever you are good at. When you remember that, pride in yourself goes right out the window. You have nothing to brag about.

Be cautious also about judging or dismissing others' gifts. That is displeasing to God and it damages relationships with others. Remember that everyone must work together to make this world work. All gifts and talents are important to accomplishing God's work. So don't brag about your own talents and don't dismiss anyone else's.

Instead, thank God for the multitude of gifts he gives. Thank him for your own gift. Thank him for others' gifts and for how they all connect to accomplish life and ministry for him.

Humility Wins

I am nothing without what you have given me.
Nothing.
What would I be except a blob of flesh without the
interests, talents and passions you put in me?
Anything that awakens my heart comes from you.

You put me where I am and gave me work to do
then you equipped me to do it.
I had nothing to do with it except the responsibility to
hone what you supplied.

Forgive me for feeling pride on any level.
How can I do that? It is completely foolish.
O God, you set me where I am. You placed me here in
This spot
For this time
With these interests and skills
To be your worker. Your woman. Your representative.

Help me remember that.
I confess my pride to you. I'm so sorry for it.
Please take it away. All of it.
Convict me of any dismissive attitude toward anyone
else's work or passions or talents you gave them.
We are all necessary.
We are all important.
We are all yours and here to do your work.
Yours – the work you put before each of us and for
which you have given us the talents we need.

Two people are better off than one,
for they can help each other succeed.

Ecclesiastes 4:9

Teamwork

A hug from a friend. Tears shared. Laughter shared. Working together. Creating together. Praying together.

Sharing life with someone makes it more meaningful. While the Lord doesn't choose to give every person a spouse, he does present opportunities for relationships through friendship. God knows how important connections are. He made us to live in community (as he does within the trinity).

What can a friend do for you? She can help you up when you're down. It's hard to cheer yourself up. She can come alongside you in a task. Work is easier and faster when shared. She can share successes with you. Cheering alone is less fun. She can open your eyes to new opportunities. We each notice different things in this world. She can encourage you to use your talents. Encouragement is a good thing.

Are you open to letting other people into your life? Do you notice the people that God brings around who are interested in you and for whom you feel some interest? Pay attention, their presence in your life is not an accident. Even if it's a little scary, be open to new relationships where you can be mutually encouraging and helpful to each other.

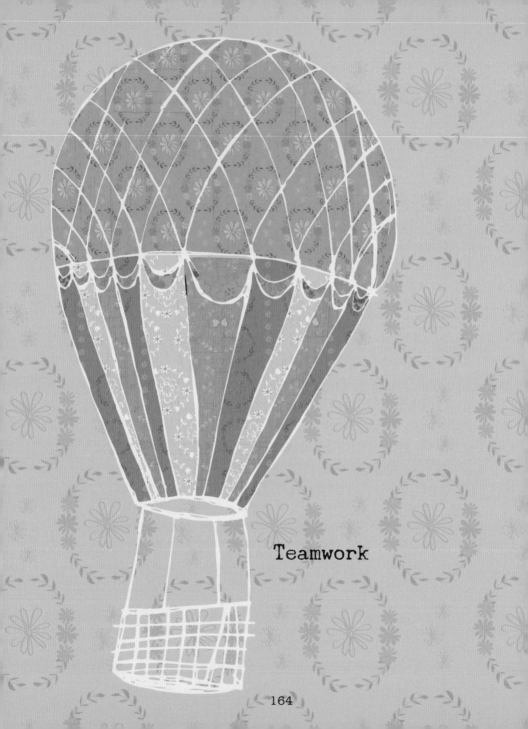

Teamwork

I do want close relationships with people who care
about me
With people I care about.
But too often I toss a roadblock in the way.
The roadblock that I'm too chicken to be vulnerable
enough to let others really know me.
I don't want them to
See my struggles
Know my weak spots.

I don't want advice, accountability, instruction or pity.
So if I keep everyone at arm's length I don't have any
of that.
I'm like an island in the ocean. An uninhabited island.
I don't have friendships with
Laughter
Tears
Help
Prayer.

But, it's ... lonely being alone.

I know I can't have it both ways.
But I'm going to need help with the old "be a friend to
have a friend" thing.
So, God ...
Help me know who to trust.
Help me know who to open up to.
Help me care so that I can be cared for.
Help me to understand the power of two over the
loneliness of one.

Yes, help me be a friend to others so that I can have
friends myself.
Two are better than one.

Don't you realize that your body is the temple
of the Holy Spirit, who lives in you and was
given to you by God? You do not belong to
yourself, for God bought you with a high
price. So you must honor God with your body.

1 Corinthians 6:19-20

Taking Care of Business

It seems like every magazine or blog tells you one more thing you SHOULD be doing. From volunteering to how to parent to devotional life to growing your own garden — everyone has great ideas but ... let's face it, you can't do them all. Of course a healthy devotional life is important. No arguing that. But, another area that can get pushed aside by women who are multi-tasking themselves crazy is ... taking care of themselves.

God gives each of us one physical body to use in this life. One. We should take care of it. Exercise, eat healthy and get enough sleep. That's basic stuff. But, there's more — use your body for good things. Do not do things that dishonor God.

God's Spirit lives in you. So, don't take him places where you would never in a million years take Jesus if he were walking around with you in the flesh. It's sobering to think that he goes everywhere with you. He hears what you say and even what you think.

Honor God by taking care of your body and using it to do good, honest, helpful, God-serving things. Help others. Be kind. Give hugs. Praise him.

Taking Care
of Business

Your Spirit lives in me.
That is beyond my comprehension.
Well, actually I don't think about it very often.
If I did I'd sure be more careful about what I put in
my mouth and where I let my feet take me.
And, I do try to take care of me.
The problem is that in my busy life everyone else's
Needs
Wants
Demands
Come before mine.
So at the end of the day, actually throughout the
day, I'm pooped.
So I grab a bite of whatever food is handy.
My best exercise is bending down to empty the
washing machine.

I don't think much about how I'm living until
I hear
Of a friend who is deathly ill
Or someone caught red-handed doing something
they wish no one had found out about.

Then the reality of the brevity of life on this blue
planet smacks me in the face.
I want to make the best of life by
Taking care of myself so I'm healthy and useable.
I want to make the best of life by
Not taking you places I wouldn't want anyone to
find out about
Or doing things I would never admit out loud.

Let's tackle this together:
Healthier living
Holier living
With this one set of skin you've given me.

"My thoughts are nothing like your thoughts," says the
LORD. "And my ways are far beyond anything you could
imagine. For just as the heavens are higher than the
earth, so my ways are higher than your ways and my
thoughts higher than your thoughts."

Isaiah 55:8-9

When You Don't Understand

Do you like to do puzzles? Have you ever tried to put a 1,000-piece puzzle together when you don't know what the final picture looks like? Not so easy. Trying to understand God's actions can be much the same. You see problems that you know only God can take care of so you pray and pray and wait. But what God chooses to do is not at all what you wanted or expected. So the bottom line becomes ... Do you trust him? Do you really trust him?

The thing is that God sees a much bigger picture than you do. He can see how this specific circumstance impacts one farther down the road. He can see how other people are touched, taught and impacted by what is happening to you — perhaps even people you don't know. He knows what you need to learn and how this circumstance can teach you. Life is far more complicated and interwoven than your human mind can comprehend. So ... do you trust him to do what's best for you and for everyone you care about? Do you trust his big-picture view with plans and goals more complex than you can even dream? Do you trust him when you are in the dark?

The world is a lot bigger than what I can see.
I know that.
I forget that.
When life gets hard and I want the pain to stop
I don't understand why you don't just fix things.
You hear my prayer.
You care.
So, just fix it ...
I forget there are connecting dots down the road that
will grow my faith deeper than I can imagine.
But that growth does not come without pain –
No pain
No gain.
Do I want to grow?
Do I want to learn?
Do I want to know you better?
Yes, of course.
But does it have to be so hard?
However, struggle is part of all the creation you've made.
Aren't trees actually strengthened by strong winds that
bend them nearly to the ground?
Aren't diamonds formed by the pressure of the earth?
God, I believe you want my faith to grow.
I want that, too.
So, I will trust your decisions
Even when they disappoint me.
I choose to believe you are doing what's best for me
Because you see a bigger picture and the end result can
be a better, stronger, more godly me.
What more could I want?

When You Don't
Understand

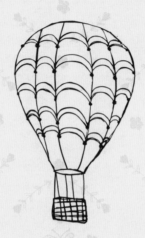

This is the day the LORD has made.
We will rejoice and be glad in it.

Psalm 118:24

Good Day/Tough Day

When the sun is out, the flowers are blooming, you've got everything you need and all things are going well you joyfully praise God and sing his goodness. Sure, it's easy to give him the credit for those good days.

What's your reaction when life gets tough? When the car has a flat tire and rain is falling in sheets and you're late to work, do you think, "God made this day?" When the doctor calls to say the test result is bad news, does that feel like a day the Lord made? When the children misbehave and disobey, is God in that day, too? When your spouse says, "I quit" and walks away ... when the pink slip comes ... when you can't pay the bills, are those God-made days? If God is in control of one kind of day he is also in control of the other. Can you rest in his love while praising him? Can you trust in his plan? Can your faith grow in the darkness? Yes, it can.

It's easy to rejoice when things are going great. The test of your faith comes in the dark times. Can you rejoice then simply because you know God is in control? His plan is larger than just this moment. He is working out his plan for you. He is God.

Good Day/Tough Day

This day? Really?
I should rejoice in the muck of this day?
I try ... but the words come out empty and
meaningless.
Because
I want my way.
I want things easy and happy and successful
I want you to do what I want.
But ... easy isn't always best
So I choose to rejoice in the love that surrounds me
I rejoice in the loneliest of moments
I rejoice in the successes of my day
I rejoice in the failures
I rejoice in the bloom of good health
I rejoice in the weakness of disease
I rejoice in the times I feel most close to you
I rejoice in the times you seem a million miles away
I rejoice in the understanding of your work
I rejoice when I haven't got a clue what you're doing
I rejoice in the knowledge and experience of your love
I rejoice when I'm not certain you even know my name
I rejoice when others treat me well
I rejoice when I'm bullied and hurt.

I will choose to rejoice even in THIS day
Because in my heart I am sure of your love.
Even when I can't feel it
I choose to trust it
I choose to rejoice whatever this day brings.

The LORD is my strength and my song; he has
given me victory. This is my God,
and I will praise him - my father's
God, and I will exalt him!

Exodus 15:2

Super Power Strength

Defeat is one of the biggest enemies of faith. Defeat makes you feel that you can't go on. It tells you there is no hope. It says no one cares. Satan uses defeat to make you give up. He uses it to tell you "the whole God-loves-you thing" is a lie. Defeat saps every ounce of strength you have. It knocks you to your knees with no resources to pick you up.

Defeat is real but there is an answer to it. Remember your God. Remember that his power created the world from nothing. Remember that his strength controls the most powerful storms. Remember that his strength made the sun stand still, helped a young boy defeat a giant, gave a sick woman the courage to reach through the crowd and touch the hem of Jesus' robe. His strength heals the sick. His strength raised Jesus back to life. His strength is in you. Yes, it's there. Call on him. Ask his help. Watch for his answer. Sense his strength welling up inside of you. Use it. You will have victory because God's strength is yours!

I've looked for strength in so many places
Wrong places.
And sometimes I found just enough faux strength to
make me linger a bit ...
A bit too long.
When that faux strength weakened or failed me then I
Crashed and burned
Discouraged and tired and hopeless.
I couldn't go on. I didn't even want to try.

Why do I look for strength from other sources?
Why am I so foolish?
The strength you give, my strong Lord, is the only true
strength.
Your strength picks me up when I'm flat on the floor in
exhaustion.
Your strength tells me I can take one more step
Resist temptation one more time
Have the backbone I need
Make the right choices
Keep on going.
Your strength helps me keep on keeping on.

Thank you that your strength is constant and steady.
Thank you that your strength puts a rod in my back
helping me stand straight and tall.
Thank you that your strength clears my foggy mind.
Thank you that your strength keeps me moving.
Thank you that your strength gives me courage.
Thank you that your strength, in me, gives me a song
that bursts from my lips in praise to you.

Super Power
Strength

How precious are your thoughts about me, O God.
They cannot be numbered!

Psalm 139:17

Precious Love

God thinks about you. That in itself is amazing. What's even more amazing (and telling) is that he doesn't just think about you when you disobey or do something that doesn't please him. He isn't just thinking stuff like, "I wish she would read the Bible more" or "Why does she say she loves me but then does stuff like that?" He loves you and he thinks loving thoughts about you. He may think about how he loves spending time with you or how proud he is of the person you are becoming. He thinks about you all the time – too often to even be able to count how often your name runs through his thoughts. You could say that God has a healthy obsession with you!

There is another way to think about this verse and that is to think how it makes you feel to know that God thinks about you. Is it a precious thought? Does it warm your heart to know you are on God's mind? Does it make you feel loved and secure? It should. Because God is thinking precious thoughts about you. He has such precious love for you.

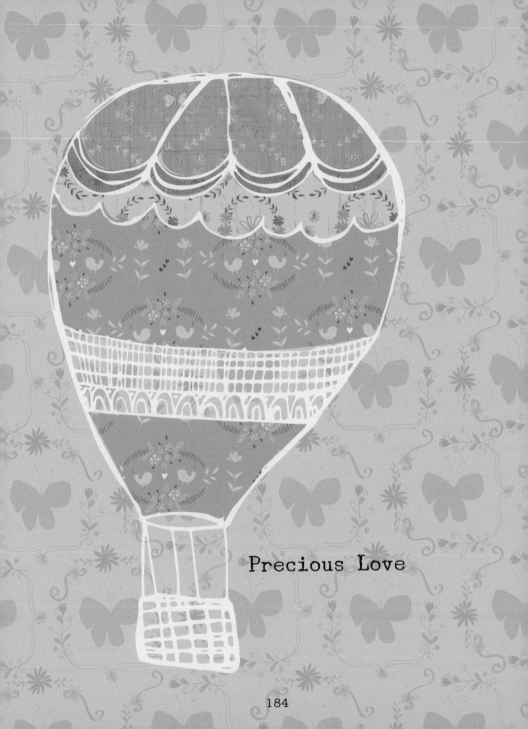

Precious Love

A million thoughts run through my mind each day
How many are about you, my God?
I think about my family, friends, job, enemies, plans ... so
many things other than you.

But you ... think about me.
I'm blown away to know that God of Creation
God who is taking care of this entire planet
God who sees us kill one another in the name of ... what?
God who sees babies enter this life
God who sees people leave this life
God who celebrates with the joyous
God who has compassion on the hurting
God who hears a bazillion prayers for help and healing
God who sees children dying of hunger
God who comforts mothers watching their children suffer
God of ... everything ... thinks about me.

Forgive me for too often pushing you aside.
Forgive me for not being more insistent on my day
my schedule, my thoughts including you.

Thank you for loving me enough to think about me.
Thank you for thinking I'm that special.
It makes me love you even more.

"Though your sins are like scarlet, I will
make them as white as snow. Though they
are red like crimson, I will make
them as white as wool."

Isaiah 1:18

No Grudges

God does not hold grudges. When you mess up, even in the most horrific way imaginable, if you tell him about it and ask for his forgiveness – he forgives. He not only forgives your sin, he cleans up your heart and life. Totally clean, not a spot of stain left over. You have a fresh start with no evidence of what you did before. How can he do this?

His heart cleaning and forgiveness are possible only because of the supreme sacrifice of his son. Jesus' torturous death was for you. He took your punishment. He paid the price for your sins. He was your blood sacrifice. Does this seem extreme? It was. But, it was necessary in order to make a personal relationship with the perfect God a possibility. You couldn't have a relationship or even dream of eternity in heaven without his sacrifice. God's forgiveness would not have been possible without Jesus' death and resurrection.

So each time you confess your sins and receive his forgiveness, remember to thank him for Jesus' sacrifice that made your new start, your cleaned-up heart, possible and for his love for you – the reason he did it all.

No Grudges

My heavenly Father
The reality of your love is shaking me to the core.
You sent your son ... your ONLY son to this earth to
live and teach and suffer and die.
And while he did that for "the world" what is swelling
my heart is that he did it for me.

The pain you must have felt juxtaposed with the love
you must have felt – I can't begin to imagine.
Such a horrendous experience because of such
Magnificent love.
Love that goes on and on.
I mess up and you love me.
I ignore you and you love me.
I come to you begging forgiveness and promising to
Never again do that thing and you forgive and forget
that sin.
Even if I do that a hundred times for that very same
sin, you forgive me and wash it away – no stain –
No memory.

Thank you. Thank you.
Father, don't ever let me take it lightly.
Remind me that it came with a cost. A cost I could
never repay.

I ask that your Spirit speak loudly into my heart so
that when I'm tempted to disobey, I will be reminded
of the cost of the forgiveness I will come begging for
and the love that makes it all possible.

The Holy Spirit helps us in our weakness.
For example, we don't know what God wants
us to pray for. But the Holy Spirit prays
for us with groanings that cannot
be expressed in words.

Romans 8:26

Aching Hearts

Another school shooting. Our world is sick. So sick. How can we understand why children are killed? Lives cut short before they have really begun. How can we comfort parents whose hearts are destroyed? How do we even pray? What do we say?

Sometimes it's hard to find the right words to pray. When such horrific things happen we may be tempted to pray for things that are almost revenge (OK, they are revenge) on the perpetrators. Is that what God wants? We want to pray for comfort for those who have been so deeply hurt. But what will truly comfort a mother or father buried in grief?

When we cannot find the words to pray ... when we may not even know how to pray ... the Holy Spirit will pray for us. He feels the cries of our hearts. He knows we agonize for lives lost, lives grieving, and even for lives destroyed by their own cruel acts. He knows we want to cry out for comfort and peace. He knows. He will translate our hearts' groanings into prayers to God. Let your heart feel. Trust the Holy Spirit to translate.

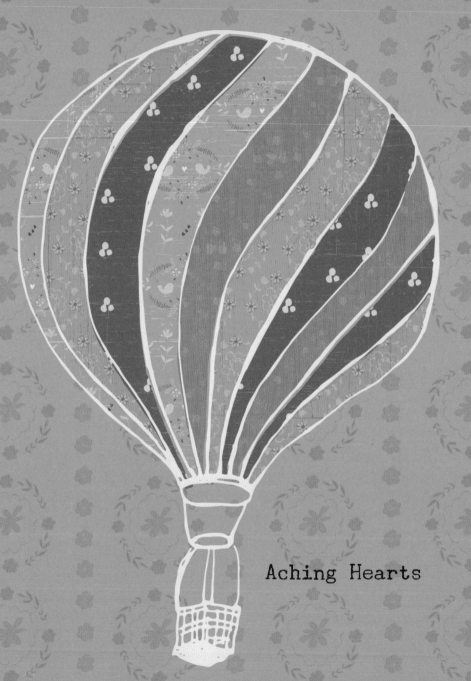

Aching Hearts

O, dear God
Why again?
Why children?
Why do those who have some sick, perverted point to
make ... some message they feel compelled to deliver ...
Why must they attack children?
What does that prove?

Young lives violently ended before they have started
living ... for what purpose?
This violence does not make a point, does it?
It only breaks hearts
So many hearts.

O God
Help us. Help this mass of fallen humanity
We need you to
Give comfort to heart-crushed parents whose very souls
are bleeding
Give grace to frightened children whose friends are no
more.

Fill us with an urgency to pray
Even when we don't know what to pray.

Your Spirit, Lord, your Spirit knows what to pray
For the broken-hearted
For the fearful
For the mind-sick perpetrators
For their families, too, who must live with what one of
their own has done.

We pray, Lord, we pray for
your Spirit to pray with us, for us, about us.

Don't sin by letting anger control you.
Don't let the sun go down while you are still angry.

Ephesians 4:26

Get Rid of Anger

Do you ever wake up angry and you don't know what you're angry about? It's hard to get over it because you don't know what caused it. But it sure colors your day. The way you interact with your children starts at the "I've had about enough" level. Words are spit out that are short and ugly. Things are laid down with a little more power than needed. A few too many cookies, chips, ice cream is consumed. Anger. Nothing good comes from it.

What causes anger? Frustration that others don't live by your agenda? Disappointment? Some anger is righteous, of course. But most anger is based in selfishness. Whether it's righteous or selfish, anger must be handled. Letting anger ride just builds bigger, uglier walls inside you and in relationships. It controls you, your responses and your attitudes. That's why God said, "Stop it." Stop anger. Talk it out. Pray it through. Let it go. Get over it. No good comes from anger. Have you seriously ever changed someone's mind by your anger? Maybe you've beaten them into submission or they've changed their actions or mind just to shut you up. But, did you "win a battle and lose the war" in that particular relationship? It's not worth it. Jesus said, "Love each other. That's what I want you to do." Get rid of anger. Come to some agreement you can live with. Let it go.

Get Rid of Anger

I've won a million arguments — said exactly the right thing at just the right time ...
But only in my mind.
I spend a lot of time rehashing disagreements or bad situations in my mind. That's when I think of what I should have said or how those words would have won. Yeah and now I realize that all that thinking time is my anger controlling me.
It occupies my thoughts and I get more angry and want to get even and have trouble being civil to that "Enemy" I've been beating up in my thoughts.

No love in that, is there, God?
Sometimes life is all about me.
What I want, feel, believe is important.
And your command to love others is buried in that me-ness.

It isn't how I want to be. In fact, it makes me tired.
So first ... please forgive me.
Then ... help me
To "get over" myself
To not demand my way all the time
To think about how I make others feel
To understand that everyone is fighting their own battle.

Help me to be more about loving and less about winning.
Help me to let go of anger.

I am overwhelmed with joy in the Lord my God!
For he has dressed me with the clothing of
salvation and draped me in a robe of
righteousness. I am like a bridegroom
dressed for his wedding or a bride
with her jewels.

Isaiah 61:10

Wedding Prep

Weddings are such fun. The planning. The anticipation. Beautiful flowers. Romantic music. The bride has a beautiful wedding gown, gets her hair and makeup done. Close friends and family gather to celebrate. Yes, it is all well thought through. But, the clothing ... well, the bride and groom's clothing is so important. It helps them look their best. It's special. Very special. More than likely these outfits will never be worn again. They are only for this special day for this special ceremony. Once in a lifetime clothing for the happiest day of your life.

You should feel just that special when you think about the beautiful gown of righteousness that God designed especially for you. Yes, it's designer clothing. It's pure and clean. It's special. It's beautiful. How cool is that?

The gown that God designed for you when you were saved presents you pure and clean and beautiful in his eyes. It is evidence of his saving grace. Wearing your beautiful salvation gown should fill you with joy beyond belief. Gratitude beyond that joy. Celebration that goes on for eternity.

Wedding Prep

You love me, God. You really love me.
You designed this special salvation gown for me so when
you look at me you don't see
My all-about-me pride
My raging jealousy
Or
My lazybones-don't-want-to-try ethic
My "I'll pray tomorrow-when-I-feel-like-it" devotion habit.

You see me clean
You see me pure
You see me saved
And coming to your heaven
You see me as your own ...
In the journey to know you better
To be more like you
To serve you.

Thank you for grace
Thank you for forgiveness
Thank you for second chances
Fresh starts
Thank you for your Spirit living in me
Teaching
Guiding
Stopping
Starting
That's true guidance.

Joy. Celebration. Gratitude. Relief.
Peace. Humility. Love.
That's how I feel about my salvation.

If you need wisdom, ask our generous God,
and he will give it to you. He will not
rebuke you for asking. But when you ask
him, be sure that your faith is in God
alone. Do not waver, for a person with
divided loyalty is as unsettled as a
wave of the sea that is blown and
tossed by the wind.

James 1:5-6

Pendulum Pray-er

Are you a pendulum pray-er? Does your trust swing from one side to the other – sometimes to God and then sometimes back to something else? Some people are crisis Christians. When they have a need (read a problem where they need God's help) they quickly swing to God and passionately pray. But even as they seriously pray about a crisis, they don't truly expect (read believe) that God will answer. Instead they swing back to trusting in friends or money or a myriad of other things to solve their problems.

God says that when you pray, you should believe that he will answer. If you try to cover your bases by praying but then swing back to putting your faith in other things, well, that won't do you much good.

God will not be an add-on to other solutions. Don't be a pendulum pray-er. You can ask God for whatever is on your heart. He wants to know. So then, trust that he hears. Trust that he will answer in the way that is best for you and all involved. You will experience more peace and your prayers will be much more effective!

Pendulum Pray-er

Prayer is hard.
No wait, it isn't prayer that's hard
Trusting is hard.
I try but I'm not very good at it.
Your Spirit lives inside me. So you already know
what I'm thinking.
But that's not enough, you want me to actually tell
you what I
Feel
Think
Hope for
Worry about.
You want me to talk to you
Which is, of course, prayer.

I do pray.
I pray and pray
But sometimes it doesn't seem that you're working or ...
Maybe even paying attention.
That's my secret fear.
I fear I'm not worthy of your time.
That's why I often grab my prayers back to take care
of things myself or by trusting friends or money or
power or ... whatever.
Yes, my trust swings back and forth between you and
whatever else looks powerful at the moment.

I want to trust you completely, God.
I want to patiently wait for you to work because
I believe you will in your time and for my good.

Give me the strength to let go
The strength to be weak because you are strong.

We can rejoice, too, when we run into problems
and trials, for we know that they help us
develop endurance. And endurance develops
strength of character, and character
strengthens our confident
hope of salvation.

Romans 5:3-4

Dealing with Change

Living is a journey. Sometimes it's a fun journey. Sometimes not so much. Journey by its very nature means change. New experiences. New scenery. New people. New jobs. Sometimes those changes are like the growing pains that the physical body goes through as it matures. Some hurt. Some keep you up at night. Growth is not easy, but it does help us mature.

If this scenario is true of physical growth then it makes sense that it's also true of spiritual growth. Stretching spiritual muscles can be just as painful and can lead to sore muscles, too.

So what's the point? You have to look for the good that comes from spiritual growing pains. Look for what you learn and how you mature. Notice how you become a better Christ-follower by what you've learned.

And, even something that may be hard once in a while, but is also good – be thankful for change and the pain of growing. Growth may be painful at times, but it's a lot more rewarding than staying in the same place, at the same maturity for your whole life. How boring would that be?

Dealing with Change

My heart is bruised.
I've been through the mill lately, God.
But then, you know that.
Changes in my life have jerked me from one side to
the other.
I can't find my footing. I've lost my equilibrium.
You know about the problems.
Maybe you orchestrated some of them.

I'm supposed to praise you for this, aren't I?
The Bible tells me to rejoice over problems.
I don't feel like it.
I'm scared. I'm hurt. I'm alone.
Friends are staying away like I've got the plague.
Family don't know what to do with me.
My bruised heart keeps me from feeling too much
because it hurts when anything touches it.

Why does this have to be? Am I growing?
Will I come out on the other side a better
Woman
Christian
Friend
Family member?

I pray that these battered heart muscles grow stronger
but not crusty so that I can't feel with others.
I pray that I come through with a better understanding
of you
But not so self-centered I can't feel for others.
Grow me through your Word
Teach me through your Holy Spirit
Change me through the changes that come from you.

Make allowance for each other's faults,
and forgive anyone who offends you.
Remember, the Lord forgave you,
so you must forgive others.

Colossians 3:13

Forgiving Others

If only we could as willingly forgive others as we want them to forgive us. If only. Too often when we hurt someone we meekly say, "Oh, I'm sorry. Really didn't mean to … blah blah blah … forgive me? Thanks. Buh-bye." So things should be fine.

But when we're on the other side of the hurt scenario, the story can go differently. The offender apologizes and our response is along the lines of, "Yeah, well, you're going to have to do a whole lot better than just say you're sorry. I need blood. I need penance. I need …" You get the idea and OK, maybe that's a little extreme.

God forgives us for the same failures over and over. He forgives us when we blatantly sin, without even considering his feelings. Because he loves us, he gives us second, third, tenth and to infinity chances. He asks us to give that same kind of forgiveness to others – to recognize that people have bad days, make bad decisions, are sometimes selfish and mean. Sometimes it's a one-time thing, sometimes it's just who people are. But not forgiving them just eats up our own guts and does nothing to them except wreck any chance for a relationship. So … thank God for forgiving you, forgive others and give them another chance, and get on with life.

Forgiving Others

I mostly do not have big sins to confess and for which I
must beg your forgiveness.
At least not big measured by what I consider big.
Convenient of me to have my own measuring stick,
Right?

No, no, not big. Just constant, piddly infractions
The same ones over and over and over.
But even with my generous attitude toward my own sin
I recognize your forgiveness. I appreciate it.
Thanks for not holding my sin against me.
Even though my sins are constant, they are not
(generally) on purpose.

Thanks for cleaning me up.
Thanks for fresh starts each day.
Thanks that your love isn't dependent on me.

The thing is — I'm not so generous with my forgiveness.
I don't want to forget. I want to make 'em pay.
I will not trust again. No second chances here.
I require bone-crushing grief and penance for hurts
done to me.
Otherwise — one and done.

I know. I know. That's not at all fair —
Asking for what I refuse to give
Receiving what I do not deserve
Holding out for what I am not required to give
Refusing to give what I am so generously blessed with.

Forgiveness. Plain and simple forgiveness.
Help me to give it as you have given it to me.

Let all that I am praise the LORD, with my whole
heart, I will praise his holy name.
Let all that I am praise the LORD;
may I never forget the good
things he does for me.

Psalm 103:1-2

Full-Time Praise

Praise springs from the heart. It is a response to who God is and what he does for you. Praise comes from recognizing God's presence in your life each day. Praise should not just happen during the worship set at a worship service. Praise should be part of everyday life.

Praise is more than "Yay God" words. It's more than singing praise choruses. Praise for God is shown by how you take care of yourself. It's shown by how you eat, exercise and rest. Your entire being praises him. Praise is caring for others, sharing their lives, helping where you can, treating them with respect. Praise is loving others as God does.

This praise explodes from your heart when you step back and recognize all that God does for you each day. His blessings. His gifts. His love. His protection. His Word. His promises. The good goes on and on.

The psalmist cautioned himself to never forget all that God has done for him. Pray the same for yourself — do not take life and it's blessings for granted. It all comes from God. Praise him with all of you all the time.

Full-Time Praise

You are the God who wakes me each morning
And blesses me with a new day to enjoy.
You are the God who makes the sun to shine,
It's light filtering through trees making lace patterns on
my window.
You are the God who sends the rain, the drops tickling
my skin even as they water your earth.
You are the God who made the rainbow stretch across the
sky so beautiful in its colorful promise.

You are the God who blesses with music to cheer my
heart and comfort my soul.
You are the God whose generosity gives talents and
passions and interests, which give purpose to my days.

You are the God who loves me through those who
love me
Whose touch is felt in the embrace of my friend
Whose strength is seen in the commitment of my spouse
Whose smile is seen in the face of my child.

You are the God who gave his Word
Written and translated and persecuted but ...
It survived
And it feeds me, comforts me, blesses me, teaches me.

You are the God who loves me completely, perfectly,
unconditionally.

And I praise you with all my heart.

All Scripture is inspired by God and is useful
to teach us what is true and to make us
realize what is wrong in our lives. It
corrects us when we are wrong and
teaches us to do what is right.
God uses it to prepare and equip
his people to do every good work.

2 Timothy 3:16-17

Instruction Book or Love Letter?

When you get a new, up-to-date piece of technology that does more than you can begin to understand, the instructions become a teaching tool to help you know how to use your new toy. That's pretty important. The inspired Word of God – the Bible – is also an Instruction Book. God provides what you need to learn as you grow in learning how to live for him and with others. If you follow what the Bible teaches you are equipped to live in this world for him. It is a process, like any learning experience but you do have this Instruction Book to give guidelines. That's helpful.

But, the Bible isn't just an Instruction Book. The whole reason God wrote it is because he loves you. So, it is also a love letter. God gives instructions on the ways to live that will please him and serve him and make life with other humans better. However, it's not a "do this or else" kind of letter, it's a "do this and you'll make the world a better place and enjoy life more" kind of letter. That's love. Instruction and love.

Instruction Book or
Love Letter?

O God, I am just a child
A child who is learning about this life.
A child who is
Longing to know you more deeply
Striving to serve you better
Hoping to obey you more completely.

You made it as easy as you could.
You gave an Instruction Book
That is not just a list of rules. (I might have ignored
that or given up when I couldn't achieve perfection.)
Your Book is infused with love – your love for me.

It shows me how you have worked with your people
Loved them, guided them, protected them.
It tells me how you want all people to know you.
I learn from it the consequences of ignoring you.

Your beautiful words, if learned and obeyed
will make this life more pleasant
More blessed, more meaningful.

Your words, if taken to heart, will show me how to
be more like you and in that be more obedient to you
More useful to you.

Your word is a lamp to my feet – guiding my steps to
righteousness.
Your word is light on my path – so I will not stumble
and fall.
Your word is a letter of love from my Creator, my God.
Thank you for it.

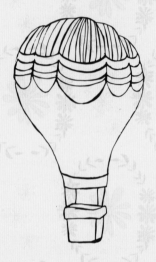

Let us think of ways to motivate one another
to acts of love and good works.

Hebrews 10:24

Unique Individual

Encouragement is important, isn't it? It helps you believe in yourself, which motivates you to more freely exercise your talents and gifts.

The thing is that everyone is different. (Thank the Lord. How boring would things be if we all had the same personalities, talents and interests?) God made every person unique so the way we encourage one another may take some thought.

We must be intentional about mentioning another's gifts and talents. A simple, "I love to hear you sing" or "You really have a gift for noticing when I'm down" or "I always learn something when you teach Bible lessons." It's an easy thing to encourage others to use their gifts.

But perhaps there is more to this verse than just encouragement. Could it be a reminder to "give each other a kick in the pants to get busy?" There are so many people who need Jesus. So many who need comfort, help, food, jobs ... the list goes on and on. We must encourage one another to pay attention and stay engaged in doing good works and loving as God does. We each have different gifts and we notice different things. Work together. Encourage each other. Learn from each other. Make a difference.

Unique Individual

We live in an ever-darkening world of selfishness and
hatred
And crimes too unspeakable to think about.

The world needs Jesus.
Plain and simple. He's the only answer to the darkness.
And yet, too often, we keep the story of Jesus' love to
ourselves.
We fear rejection
Or derision
So we keep our mouths shut and wait for someone else
to tell the news, even though we know you have
uniquely gifted each of us to use in certain ways
to certain people at certain times.

We could be your people who make a difference
By sharing your love
We could take a stand for you and begin to turn this
world back to you.
We could start — one voice at a time to one person at a
time.
We could encourage each other with a
Pat on the back
Or a "You can do this"
Or a simple prayer for strength.

We can make a difference.
One voice at a time. One voice that becomes ten
A hundred
A thousand
And on and on.
Working together, encouraging one another.
Sharing your love. Changing our world.

Has the LORD ever needed anyone's advice?
Does he need instruction about what is good?
Did someone teach him what is right or show
him the path of justice? No, for all the
nations of the world are but a drop in the bucket.
They are nothing more than dust on the scales.
He picks up the whole earth as though it
were a grain of sand.

Isaiah 40:14-15

God's Greatness

Perhaps you've heard the little rhyme, "My God is so big, so strong and so mighty. There's nothing my God cannot do!" Children recite those words as they do hand motions. It's cute. And they have no idea how true and how powerful those words are. It may be that we adults do not fully appreciate their truth either.

God NEEDS nothing from anyone or anything. There is nothing individuals or nations or people or planets can do for him that he can't do for himself. His knowledge and power are beyond human comprehension.

There is no denying that our world is in a mess. Morals, attitudes, love, humility and a zillion other things are spiraling downward. But God is greater than all of that. He is greater and more powerful than any nation or peoples. No situation or war or hatred is hopeless because ultimately it is God who is in control over all. God is God. It is comforting and good to remember that. He is in control. He knows how things will turn out.

If we truly grasped your greatness, would we not
quickly submit to you?
Your will
Your time
Your power
Your choices.
We would submit in relief that you are in
Powerful control.

Our world is a cacophony of wickedness ...
Crimes
Atrocities
Wars
Disasters
Terrorists
Each one shouting louder than the one before until
our broken and fearful hearts can take no more.

But your power and might, O God, surpasses all.
You could take down nations with a whisper of your
breath.
You could fell the most evil among us.
Nothing can stand before you. Nothing.

Thank you that you are in control.
Thank you that your power and strength are couched
in the love of your hopes for the salvation of all
mankind.

God's Greatness

This is my command – be strong and courageous!
Do not be afraid or discouraged. For the
LORD your God is with you wherever you go.

Joshua 1:9

Need to Be Strong

Do you sometimes get tired of being strong? The need to be strong can be constant and pretty lonely. It can wear you down. Whether you need strength in living for Christ in a world that doesn't want you to or being a strong parent or trying to move forward in a career dominated by men or being single in a couple's world ... whatever it is that you need strength for ... it is tiring.

Trudging through the high-walled valley of whatever you're dealing with is lonely, too. There are some things your friends and loved ones can't help with. But, you aren't alone. God is with you always. Always. So when you get tired, when you feel hopeless, when you don't think you have one ounce of strength left in you, ask for his help. His strength will keep you going. His presence will remind you that you're not alone. He will give you courage to keep pressing forward to be the person, woman, worker, mom, wife, friend, Christian he knows you are capable of being. He knows all the struggles and battles you face. He sees the ones up ahead, too. None of them are too big for him.

Need to Be Strong

I'm in darkness. Deep darkness.
The air is heavy
I can't move
I'm tired but sleep evades me
My muscles ache
My breath is shallow
I am afraid.
Scared to go on
Scared to not go on.

I pretend to be strong but I'm not
It's an act – one I'm pretty good at.
Maybe I should be on Broadway since I am fooling so
many people – but you aren't buying my act.
You know I'm pretending even if no one else knows.

I need strength, O God. Strength that can come only
from you.
If I allow you into my heart and give you control
of my life and I submit my will to yours then your
strength will fill me.
If I allow it to soak into my heart, it will empower me.

You know my darkness. You know my struggles.
You have the answer and you have a plan for me.
It begins with my courage and trust
Being placed in you.
I choose courage
I choose strength
I choose you.

Live a life filled with love, following the
example of Christ. He loved us and offered
himself as a sacrifice for us,
a pleasing aroma to God.

Ephesians 5:2

Follow Your Leader

It shouldn't be that hard, should it, to live a life filled with love? It sounds easy enough. Well, it is easy to love your friends and people who live a similar lifestyle. It's harder to love people who are disagreeable or who choose living in a way you feel is totally wrong and depraved. It's easy to "say" you love them. But, would you want to hang out with them? Would you have them in your home? Would you build relationships with them? Of course there is the idea of keeping separate from the world. But, is that what Jesus did?

Nope, he hung out with sinners. He went to their homes for dinner. He got to know them. How else could they know him?

What is the verse in Ephesians saying to you? Maybe it's suggesting that you live sacrificially by spending time with people who are hard for you to love. Talk with them. Listen to them. See them. Give them a chance to know you and by that, a chance to see God's love in person. This kind of love smells good to God.

Follow Your
Leader

I long to be a great imitator of Jesus.
To be more and more like him.
I want to love like Jesus.
He wouldn't be bound by the things that limit my love.
Things like skin color, sexual preference, denominations,
financial status or any of the other standards I use to
categorize people.

I want to see the people who walk through my life each
day in the same way Jesus sees them.
Show me, God, how to look past tough exteriors to see
lonely hearts.
Help me see the insecurities that cause some to behave
badly.
Remind me of the struggles some face just to make it
through each day.
I need to feel the urgency of how much those who are
hard to love need you.
Convict me to become the pathway to them meeting you.

I don't want to take this lightly. I want to expand my
circle of love.
To love those who make me uncomfortable
To love those who make me angry
To love those who frighten me
To love those I don't understand.

To love ... like Jesus loves.

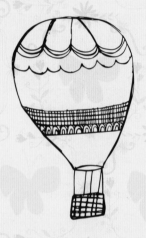

If you try to hang on to your life, you will lose it.
But if you give up your life for my sake and
for the sake of the Good News, you will
save it. And what do you benefit if you
gain the whole world but lose your own soul?

Mark 8:35-36

Important Choices

These are some pretty intense words from Jesus about trying to stay on the fence between living for him and doing whatever you want to do. That's a precarious position. Several times in his brief teaching ministry, Jesus made the point that you need to get all in or get out. You just cannot keep a foot in both worlds.

What does Jesus mean by "giving up your life for him?" Simply put – let go. Let go of your will to do what you want without obeying him. Let go of your agenda. Let go of the world's value system that defines success as power, money and fame.

It's sobering to think that if you live your life pursuing those things with all your energy, when you come to the end of life, you have nothing. Seriously ... nothing. You haven't accepted Jesus as your Savior. You've invested no energy in obeying God or serving him. So, you had a successful life by the world's standard, but you have nothing for eternity.

So, what's most important to you? Knowing God, serving him and having the assurance of eternity with him? Or power, money and fame? Choose wisely. This is important.

Important Choices

Gracious God, I acknowledge your love
Shown so generously and sacrificially through the gift of
Jesus.
You held nothing back.
You went "all in" for me.
Your sacrifice was complete and even though it must
have been hard, the pain was overshadowed by your love.

My response to your love is too often half-hearted.
I try to stay comfortable in the world but keep my heart
turned toward you.
That doesn't work so well.
I pray for strength to let go. Let completely go.
To get off the fence and be "all in" for you.
To let go of my comfy (favorite) sins
To let go of pursuits that have nothing to do with you
To commit to obeying you even when it isn't the popular
thing to do.
To love you enough to take a stand for you in a crowd of
no one else standing.
To be brave enough to stand alone if necessary.

I pray for opportunities to share you with others because
I have the courage to do so.
I pray for a tender heart that lets your love seep out to
others because I'm all yours — even to others who are
hard to love.

I pray that I will find my true life by letting go of my old
life.
True life with you and for you and because of you.

Let your roots grow down into him, and let your
lives be built on him. Then your faith will
grow strong in the truth you were taught,
and you will overflow with thankfulness.

Colossians 2:7

Good Root System

What do you know about roots? The basic thing, of course, is that a plant's nutrition comes through the roots. Both food and water are sucked up through the roots and feed even the most giant trees. It's important for roots to be in healthy soil to provide all the good stuff a plant needs. If a plant has a bad root system, the plant doesn't survive. Roots spread and grow under the ground giving plants the stability to withstand wind and rain.

Roots are important. That makes the challenge in this verse important because every person puts the roots of how they build their lives into something. The healthiest place to put your life trust is in Jesus, of course. You do that by trusting him and by getting to know him in a deeper and more intimate way. As your faith roots grow down deep into him and nutrition comes from knowing him, your faith will grow deeper and stronger all the time. It's a great system for growing stronger and deeper in your faith.

The natural response of that strong, deep faith will be thankfulness to God for making all this possible.

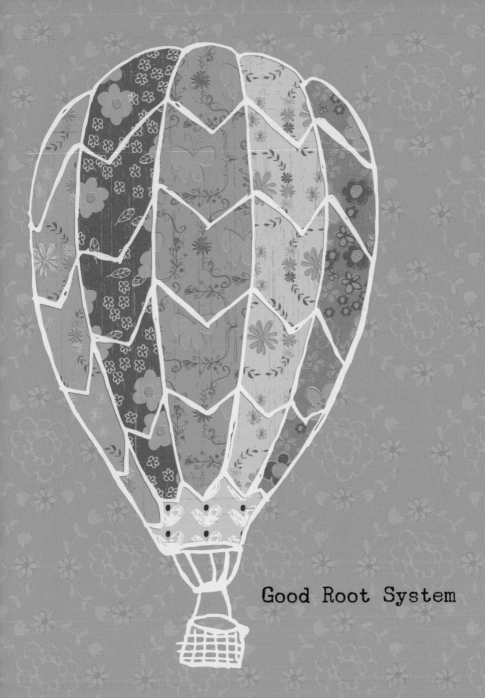

Good Root System

We are your people
We claim your name
We claim your salvation
We claim your heaven.

We are your people
Who make our own plans and ask you to bless them
Who not so humbly begin to expect your blessings.

We are your people
Who read your Word and too often see what others
need to know but not what we need to learn.

We are your people
Who lift our hands in praise when life is going well
And beg for relief when it is not.

We are your people
Striving to be like you without experiencing
perseverance through suffering.

Show us, your people, how to let go of our own
agendas so that the roots of our faith can grow
deep into you.
Help us learn to trust.
Feed us, nourish us, give us living water through
our Jesus roots.
Grow our faith stronger
Braver
Surer.
Grow our love deeper
Wider
Purer.
Grow our thankfulness
More honest and true.

He who is the faithful witness to all
these things says, "Yes, I am coming soon!"
Amen! Come, Lord Jesus!

Revelation 22:20

He Is Coming Soon!

One day this will all be over. Jesus is coming back to take his family home to heaven with him. He said that it will happen. Sometimes we forget the reality of this truth. It must be that we forget it or we would be much more urgent about telling others about Jesus. We would be heartbroken when loved ones leave this earth without knowing him.

A forever with God in heaven is real. A forever without him in hell is real, too. None of us know when that forever is going to begin. We don't know how many days we have left on this planet.

If we have accepted Jesus as Savior we have the assurance of forever in heaven. We can look forward to it, be thankful for it, celebrate it. But, we can't afford to rest while there are still people who do not have that assurance in their lives. Accepting Jesus is a personal choice but it's a choice that can't be made if people don't know about him.

Jesus is coming again. Let everyone know!

He Is Coming Soon!

We are anxious with each terrorist attack.
We wonder if we are safe, if our children and
grandchildren will have a chance to grow to adulthood.

We are bewildered by the horrific crimes of
trafficking children and prostituting little ones too
young to even know what's happening to them.

We are crushed by the natural disasters that
destroy cities, tear families apart and take away
homes and jobs.

But none of what's happening surprises you.
You saw it all before one child was taken, one
bomb exploded, one war began. You knew.

We made our choice ... well Adam and Eve made
their choice and we bear the brunt of it.
We are incapable of correcting it.
Still, we know that you could stop every terrifying thing.
You are more powerful than nations, tsunamis,
hurricanes, terrorists, traffickers.
But you let us live with the consequences of our choice –
Even as it breaks your tender heart to see
us hurt and fearful.
We live. We wait. We obey. We serve. We share.
Until Jesus comes back. He will come back and it
will all be made right.
Come quickly, Jesus. Come quickly.

Topical Index